Thinking through Language

Book One

National Council of Teachers of English
1111 Kenyon Road, Urbana, Illinois 61801

Thinking through Language

Book One

Dan Kirby

Carol Kuykendall

NCTE Advisory Committee on Publications for Students: John H. Bushman, Chair; Ouida H. Clapp; Beverly Haley; Joan Hansen; Hugh D. Rank; Shirley Wurth; Theodore Hipple, *ex officio*; Paul O'Dea, NCTE Staff Liaison.

"The Cathedral" by Auguste Rodin reproduced by permission of the Rodin Museum: Gift of Jules E. Mastbaum. Philadelphia Museum of Art. Photograph by A. I. Wyatt, Staff Photographer.

"There Will Come Soft Rains" by Ray Bradbury reprinted by permission of Don Congdon Associates, Inc. Copyright 1950 by Ray Bradbury, renewed 1978.

"There Will Come Soft Rains" by Sara Teasdale reprinted by permission of Macmillan Publishing Company from *Collected Poems* of Sara Teasdale. Copyright 1970 by Macmillan Publishing Company, renewed 1948 by Mamie T. Wheless.

Book Design: Allen Carr Design

NCTE Stock Number 25360

© 1985 by the National Council of Teachers of English. All rights reserved. Printed in the United States of America.

It is the policy of NCTE in its journals and other publications to provide a forum for the open discussion of ideas concerning the content and the teaching of English and the language arts. Publicity accorded to any particular point of view does not imply endorsement by the Executive Committee, the Board of Directors, or the membership at large, except in announcements of policy, where such endorsement is clearly specified.

Library of Congress Cataloging in Publication Data

Kirby, Dan.
   Thinking through language, book one.

   1. Creative thinking (Education)   2. Mental work.
3. Association of ideas.   4. Learning.   I. Kuykendall,
Carol, 1933–   . II. Title.
LB1062.K49   1985   370.15′2   85-13610
ISBN 0-8141-2536-0

Contents

UNIT I	Experiencing the Arts	3
UNIT II	Exploring Possibilities	35
UNIT III	Investigating the Issues	61
UNIT IV	Probing the Future	87

About This Book

During your years in school, you've had lots of books—books for reading, writing, spelling, math, science, and social studies. Right now, your locker is crammed full of textbooks. Why add to the collection?

One big reason: your collection probably doesn't include a book on thinking. In fact, this may be the first book on thinking you've ever seen.

At first, the idea of a book on thinking seems a little strange. Thinking isn't a subject in school. Certainly it's nothing new. Haven't you been thinking all your life?

Of course you have. Thinking is how you make sense of what you see and hear. It's how you remember things, dream up new ideas, and solve everyday problems. It's how you learn—in school and out. Since thinking is so important to almost everything you do, wouldn't you like to think better?

Just reading this book won't help much. Becoming a better thinker takes more than reading. It's an active process. That's why the following pages are full of things to do, activities that will sharpen your mind and help you learn how it works best. This book is an invitation to start your own mental exercise program.

Most of the exercises in this program will involve language. That's because talking and writing are ways of thinking. So are listening and reading. As you work your way through the book, you'll see why it's called *Thinking through Language*.

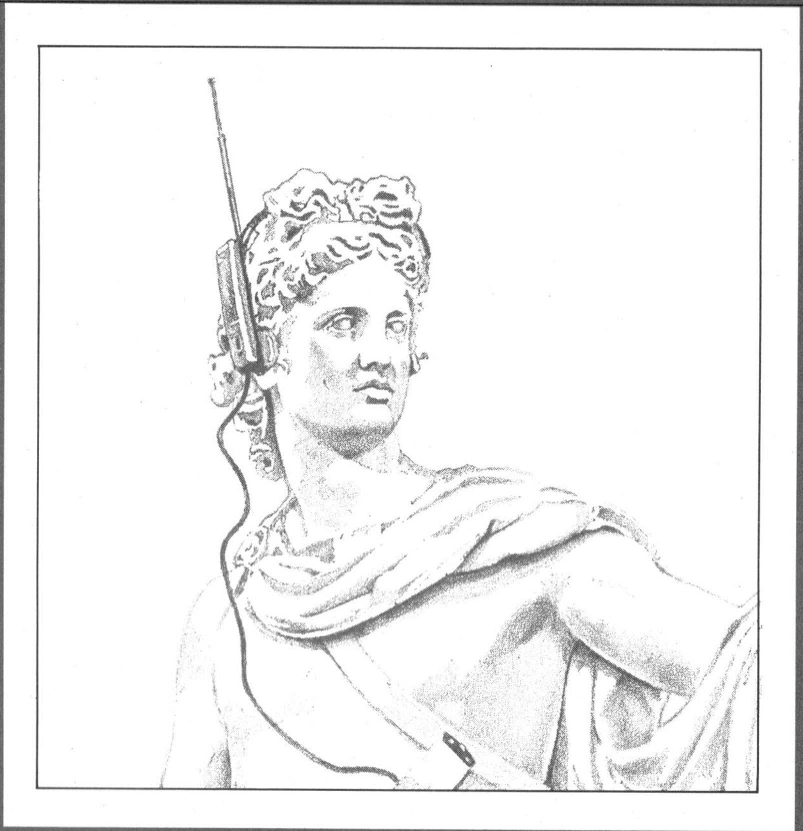

UNIT 1 Experiencing the Arts

WORDS are powerful tools for thinking, but thinking doesn't start with words. It starts with experience—with taking in what we see, hear, feel, smell, and taste. That's where this book starts. The first unit will give you lots of chances to experience the world through your senses.

Artists can teach the rest of us a great deal about this kind of thinking. Their work depends on it. One artist says: "Learning to draw is really a matter of learning to see—and that means a good deal more than merely looking through your eyes."

The activities in this unit will help you learn to see, not just look through your eyes. You will learn to think like an artist. You'll soak up experience, then recreate it in your own way. You'll have a chance to draw, make music, perform, and compose poems. At the end of the unit, you'll share your best work at a class art festival.

Collecting Yourself

Artists almost always keep a sketchbook. That's where they collect ideas in the rough. Quick, on-the-spot drawings and jottings capture a moment before it can get away. These drawings and jottings provide raw materials for more detailed work later. Keeping your own sketchbook will help you learn to think and work like an artist.

ACTIVITY

Making a Sketchbook and a Portfolio

ON YOUR OWN

Right away, find or make a sketchbook that's a handy size to carry with you. Since unlined pages are best for sketches, you might take ten or fifteen sheets of typing paper and fold them in half horizontally. Add a construction paper cover, staple firmly along the fold, and you'll have a fine sketchbook. If you prefer, you can buy one ready-made or use a tablet you already have at home. In any case, make an attractive cover. Let yourself go. Make the cover look like the artist you're about to become.

Your sketchbook is a place to save ideas. You'll also need a place to save works in progress and finished pieces. You'll need an artist's portfolio.

To make one, find two large pieces of cardboard or heavy construction paper. Just tape the sheets of cardboard or paper together on three sides to form a large pouch. Letter your name on both sides.

Paper portfolios aren't sturdy enough to carry around very much. While you and your classmates are working through this unit, you'll probably find it best to keep your portfolios at school. Try to stack them on a flat surface rather than stand them on edge.

Seeing by Drawing

So much for preliminaries. It's time to start filling that portfolio. Your first piece of work will be a drawing. Don't worry if you've never been very good at drawing. The purpose of this activity is not to produce a masterpiece. In fact, the point of the activity isn't even drawing. It's seeing.

Think about these two comments, both by successful artists:

"The painter draws with his eyes, not his hands."

"What I have not drawn, I've never seen."

Can both of these statements be true? Is seeing the basis of drawing? Or is drawing the basis of seeing? The two ideas seem contradictory. The next activity will help you check them out for yourself.

ACTIVITY

Drawing without Looking

ON YOUR OWN

You'll need a large piece of unlined paper—preferably manila—and a soft lead pencil. Secure the paper to your desktop. Be sure it won't move around. Now hold the pencil in the hand you write with, and place the point near the bottom of the paper.

Place your other hand out to one side. Turn so that you can look comfortably at that hand but not at the paper. Now you are ready to "see" your hand by drawing it.

Focus your eyes where your hand joins your wrist. Very slowly, let your eyes follow the outline of your hand—what artists call the *contour.* Notice even the tiniest curve or the slightest wrinkle on your hand. Move the pencil along. Imagine that the pencil is touching the hand and being guided by it. Let the pencil follow your eyes around the entire hand, up and down each finger, back to the wrist. Don't hurry. Don't peek at your drawing. This is a slow-motion exercise.

When you have finished, turn back around so that you can see your drawing. It may not look much like a hand. Since you couldn't see the paper, the proportions may be wrong. Lines may even run across each other. That's fine. The point of the activity isn't learning to draw. It's learning to see more carefully.

Place your hand beside your drawing:

- What parts of the drawing look most like your hand? Put an X next to those parts.
- What parts of your hand did you find easiest to draw? What parts seemed hardest? Put a checkmark next to them.
- As you were drawing, what details of your hand were most noticeable? Do they show up in your drawing?

WITH A PARTNER

Let a classmate look at both your hand and your drawing. Have that classmate tell you what part of the drawing looks most accurate. Discuss with your partner what seemed easiest and hardest to draw. Also point out what seemed most noticeable about your hand as you were looking at it. When you finish, look back at those comments by artists on page 6. Now that you've tried drawing as a way of seeing, what do you think about these comments?

When you and your partner finish, initial your drawing and date it. Put it in your portfolio for safekeeping.

Going Beyond

Try some other ways of "seeing" your hand. Here are some possibilities. You can think of others.

- Trace it.
- Draw it large, filling the whole page.
- Draw it fast, without lifting your pencil.
- Draw only a part of it.
- Copy your hand in a photocopy machine.
- Cut out a silhouette of your hand; try several different "poses."
- Coat the palm of your hand with chalk or ink from a stamp pad. Make a print by pressing on paper.
- Form a piece of floral wire into the shape of your hand.
- Clip magazine pictures of hands doing things your hands do.
- Trace your hand. Then cut out hands of various sizes and glue them inside the outline of your own. This kind of art made by gluing together a picture is called a *collage*.

Be sure to save all your creations. Put them in your portfolio to share with your teacher and classmates.

Experiencing the Arts

Thinking Hands

Hands are the artist's truest tools. Maybe that's why they are also one of the artist's favorite subjects. Just walk through any museum and you'll see abundant evidence of this fascination.

Few artists have done more with hands than the French sculptor Rodin. The next thing you'll do is study two views of one of his pieces. Since you'll be looking at photographs rather than the piece, you won't see it in three dimensions. You'll have to use your imagination. Imagining is a big part of thinking like an artist. So is looking closely at the works of other artists.

As you study the photographs and imagine how the real piece looks, keep in mind how much sculptors depend on their hands. One famous sculptor—not Rodin—always spoke of her left hand as her "thinking hand." The other, she explained, just held the hammer. The thinking hand kept her in touch with the stone.

ACTIVITY

Seeing Dimensions

ON YOUR OWN

Look closely at the pieces in these photographs:

Rodin Museum:
Gift of Jules E. Mastbaum.
Philadelphia Museum of Art.
Photograph by A. I. Wyatt,
Staff Photographer.

Can you tell that the piece is a sculpture? How would the original look. How big do you suppose it is? How would it feel to the touch?

In your sketchbook, make a list of words describing the piece. Some of your words should describe the hands themselves; others, the size, shape, texture, and color of the sculpture.

Position your hands like those in the sculpture. What does holding your hands in this position remind you of? Suggest a title for the piece.

AS A CLASS

Share your title with the class. Listen for those that carry the same idea as yours. Talk about your reasons for choosing various titles.

Seeing with the Senses

When we create things, it looks as if our hands do most of the work. But hands need more to work with than clay, paint, or ink. They need a rich store of ideas and images.

Artists collect their images by being sensitive to the physical world. That's where painters and sculptors find shapes, colors, and textures. It's where musicians find sounds. The raw material for creation is around all of us, but it's up to us to make it our own. We have to open up, tune in, and "see" in new ways. We need to experience the world through our senses. We have to soak up our environment like sensory sponges.

ACTIVITY

Sensory Tour

ON YOUR OWN OR IN A GROUP

Take your senses for a walk. Perhaps your teacher will organize a group tour or ask you to take one on your own. In either case, do the following things on your tour. Keep a record in your sketchbook. Write down a few descriptive words about each of the findings below:

1. See something smaller than your hand.
2. See something bigger than you are.
3. Hear something far away.
4. Hear something very close.
5. Feel something smooth.
6. Feel something rough.
7. Find something natural.
8. Find something made by humans.
9. Find something surprising or out-of-place.
10. Bring back several things that catch your eye.

Experiencing the Arts 9

AS A CLASS

Share what happened on your tour with your classmates. On the chalkboard, compile a class list with these headings:

- Small Things
- Nearby Sounds
- Natural Things
- Big Things
- Smooth Things
- Human-made Things
- Faraway Sounds
- Rough Things
- Surprising Things

ACTIVITY

Tabletop Composition

IN A GROUP

Choose a favorite found object from those you brought back from your walk. Show it to a small group of classmates, perhaps six or seven people. Work with the same group to make a tabletop composition—that is, a three-dimensional collage that includes each person's favorite object.

You'll need a fairly large surface—perhaps a desktop, table, or bookshelf. Take a few minutes to look at all of the objects together. Decide what effect you want to achieve in your collage. Do you want to express a theme or an idea? Or are you just interested in the way the composition will look, maybe a certain combination of color or line? Would a background or frame help? Experiment with colored paper or any other available material you think would help your composition.

Arrange all of your group's objects into a tabletop composition. Move things around until the overall effect satisfies the group. Decide on a title for the creation.

Now take your own small-group tour of the classroom and look at the compositions of other groups. Decide what you would have titled each one. Jot those titles in your sketchbook.

AS A CLASS

When the class reconvenes, check the match between the title your group gave its composition and the titles suggested by other groups. Do the titles suggest that viewers saw what you wanted them to see in your composition?

ON YOUR OWN

Before your group composition is dismantled, draw it on a large sheet of paper. Make your sketch fill the whole sheet. Don't worry about detail. Concentrate on the pattern of the objects. When you finish, put the drawing in your portfolio.

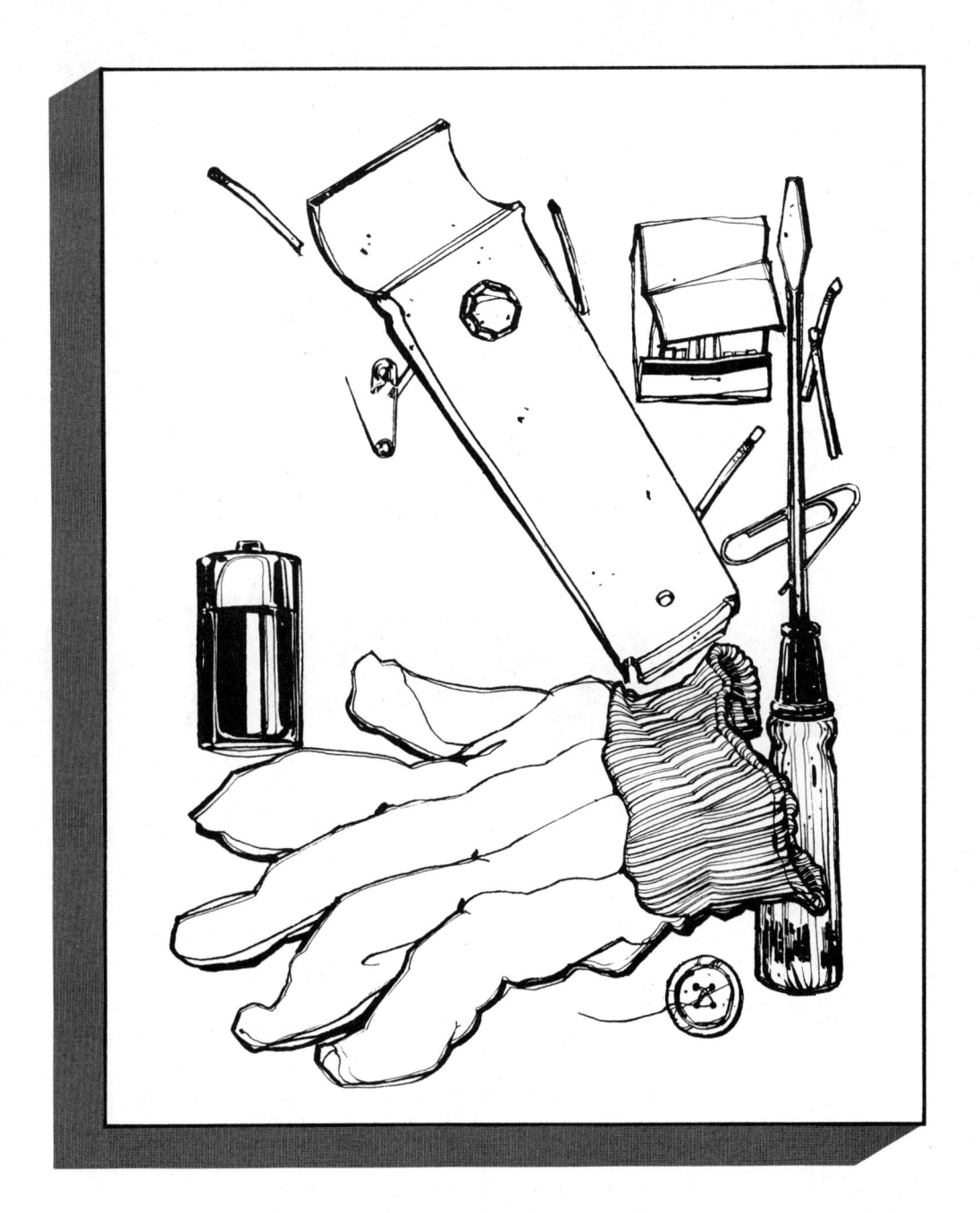

In your sketchbook, explain how and why your group arranged the objects as you did. Retracing what you did in writing will help you understand better how you take in experience through your senses, and then how you select and arrange what you have taken in. The more you learn about seeing, selecting, and arranging, the closer you'll come to thinking like an artist.

Experiencing the Arts

Going Beyond

Choose one of these activities or substitute one of your own:

- Choose images you especially liked from the sensory tour and arrange them into a list poem.
- Make a collage of rough things, small things, natural things, or surprising things.
- Make a tape of sounds like the ones heard on your walk.
- Sketch something you brought back from your walk.
- Try a "Zen drawing"—a sketch which suggests the essence of something without trying to reproduce it accurately.

Save any drawings in your portfolio. Tape or staple any writings in your sketchbook. One of your creations may be good enough to develop further and use as your entry in your class art festival.

Seeing Close Up

On your sensory tour, you went out looking for things to observe. Going on that kind of excursion is a good way to give your senses a workout. But it's not the only way. There's plenty to observe right where you are.

At the moment, that's probably a classroom. Since you've been in that room every day for weeks, you know every inch of it. Where you are right now, you couldn't possibly see anything you haven't already seen. Right?

Wrong.

Most of us don't really look at the things we see most often. We give familiar places—and even people—little more than a passing glance. We take them for granted. In a way, what is most familiar to us becomes invisible.

The challenge of the next activity is to find something new or surprising right where you are. Like a photographer, you'll explore your surroundings and search out interesting details. You'll notice color, shape, texture, and patterns. You'll be on the alert for anything unexpected or out-of-place.

ACTIVITY

Paper Camera

ON YOUR OWN

First, make your own paper camera. Take a half sheet of paper and cut or carefully tear a one-inch square out of the middle like this:

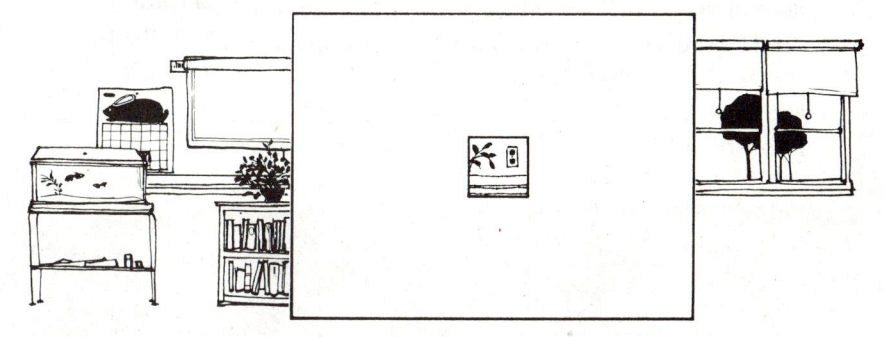

You can use the hole as a viewfinder to focus your observations on one detail at a time.

Without leaving your chair, hold your paper camera five or six inches in front of one eye. Close the other eye. Starting at one corner of the room, scan each wall. Also scan the floor, ceiling, and classroom furniture. Move slowly so that you can study each image framed in your viewfinder. Look for details you've never noticed before—for example, a mismatched floor tile, the molding around a chalkboard, a calendar still turned to last month, the metal grid shading fluorescent lights. In your sketchbook, list at least five such details. Choose one to examine closer up. Study it through the viewfinder of your paper camera and write a brief description.

Using tape, post your paper as close as possible to the feature of the classroom it describes. Then take your paper camera and tour the room. Read each description and look through your viewfinder at the feature described. How many things are you noticing for the first time?

AS A CLASS

Compile a chalkboard list of all classroom features described. Were any described by more than one person? Which seem most interesting? Most surprising? Why?

Experiencing the Arts 13

Going Beyond

Complete one of these activities or one that you choose yourself. Record results in your sketchbook to share with your teacher and classmates.

- Spend several minutes looking closely at things you wear every day: perhaps your wristwatch, jacket, jeans, and sneakers. Keep looking at each item until you find something you've never noticed before—for example, the color of numbers on a watch face, the trademark on a shirt or jeans tag, extra eyelets on the sides of your sneakers. Describe what you find.

- Do a foot-by-foot scan of your room at home as you did your classroom. Draw or describe at least three things that you find especially interesting or surprising.

- Use your paper camera to do a close-up study of patterns in familiar things around your house. Possibilities include a pebbled walkway, the grain of natural wood, a chain-link fence, the bark of a tree, the tread on a bicycle tire. Draw each pattern bigger than life.

Seeing with Words

You've already learned that "seeing" is all-important in creating. You know firsthand how important it is in the visual arts. It's just as important for artists who create with words rather than with paint, stone, or film.

For many people, words are the most difficult medium in which to create. Think about your experience in describing something you saw through your paper camera. Would drawing a picture of it have been easier? The next few activities will challenge you to do even more creative things with words.

But relax. You have plenty of raw material. You've been soaking up experiences all your life. Your head is full of mind pictures. You're going to translate those pictures into words you will like. First, you need to get comfortable, to tune in to your own mind.

ACTIVITY

Colors and Ideas

AS A CLASS

Some words are rich with pictures. Such word pictures are called *images*. This activity will help you explore connections among colors, emotions, and ideas. Your teacher will show you an assortment of colored squares. Now stare at them while your teacher reads a series of questions to you. Don't look around at your friends. Concentrate on the colors, and name the first color a question makes you think of. Ready? Concentrate! Write down answers to each question—fast.

What is your favorite color?	What color is nervous?
What color is warmest?	What color is home?
What color is coldest?	What color is school?
What color is summer?	What color is today?
What color is winter?	What color is tomorrow?
What color is sad?	What color is you?
What color is tired?	

Matching colors and ideas is a kind of thinking called *association*. Did you notice anything interesting about the associations your classmates made between colors and ideas? Was there an association that was shared by almost all students? Was there an association that almost no one agreed upon? What generalizations can you make about colors and ideas?

ACTIVITY

Mapping a Color

The feelings and associations surrounding a color can be quite personal and quite diverse. Here's a way to explore that. We asked our friend Tom to think of the color "green" and list as many associations as possible. On the next page there is a map of Tom's thoughts on green.

How many different kinds of associations do you see in this map? What guesses can you make about Tom from his map?

Experiencing the Arts

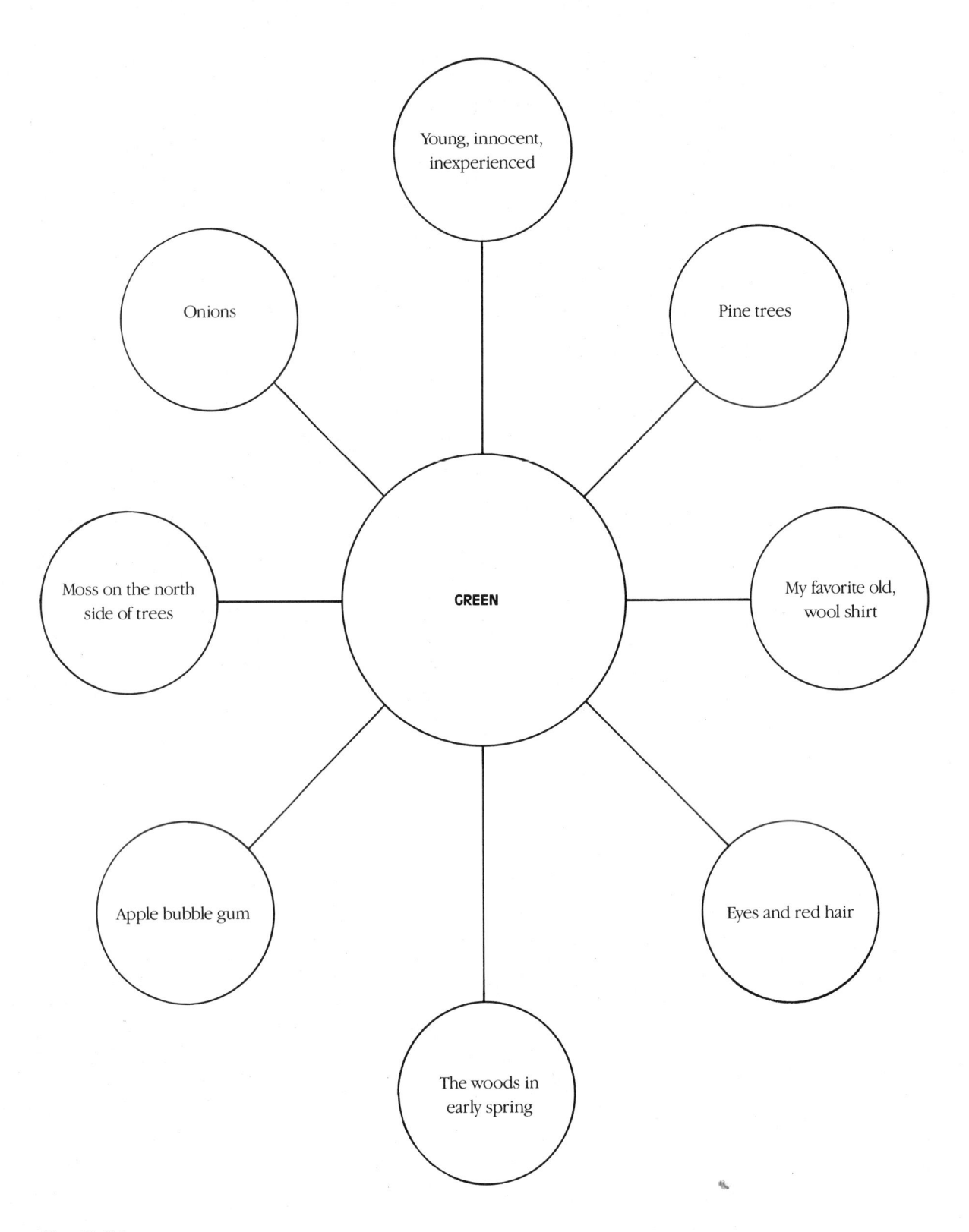

- Young, innocent, inexperienced
- Pine trees
- My favorite old, wool shirt
- Eyes and red hair
- The woods in early spring
- Apple bubble gum
- Moss on the north side of trees
- Onions

GREEN

ON YOUR OWN

Now try a color map yourself. In your sketchbook make a large map like Tom's. Make at least nine outer circles. Pick a color and then work quickly. Repeat the color to yourself, and then write down the first thing that comes into your mind. Move to the next circle and write down the next thing. Keep going until all circles are filled.

WITH A PARTNER

When you are finished, show your map to a partner. Let your partner guess what different associations show about you as a person.

Going Beyond

- Visit an auto dealer and ask to see the color selection chart for new cars. Jot down the names of all the colors. What observations can you make about car colors?

- Visit a paint store. Look at paint chips and color charts. Jot down the names of some of the more unusual colors. What observations can you make about paint colors?

ACTIVITY
Mind Maps

It's easy to find associations for colors. In fact, our minds are constantly relating things. For instance, our minds have associations for all words. If someone said *vacation* to you, lots of pleasant associations might pop up. On the other hand, if someone said *hospital,* the associations might be quite different.

Experiencing the Arts 17

One way of exploring associations is to follow a series of words to see where they take you. Look at this example:

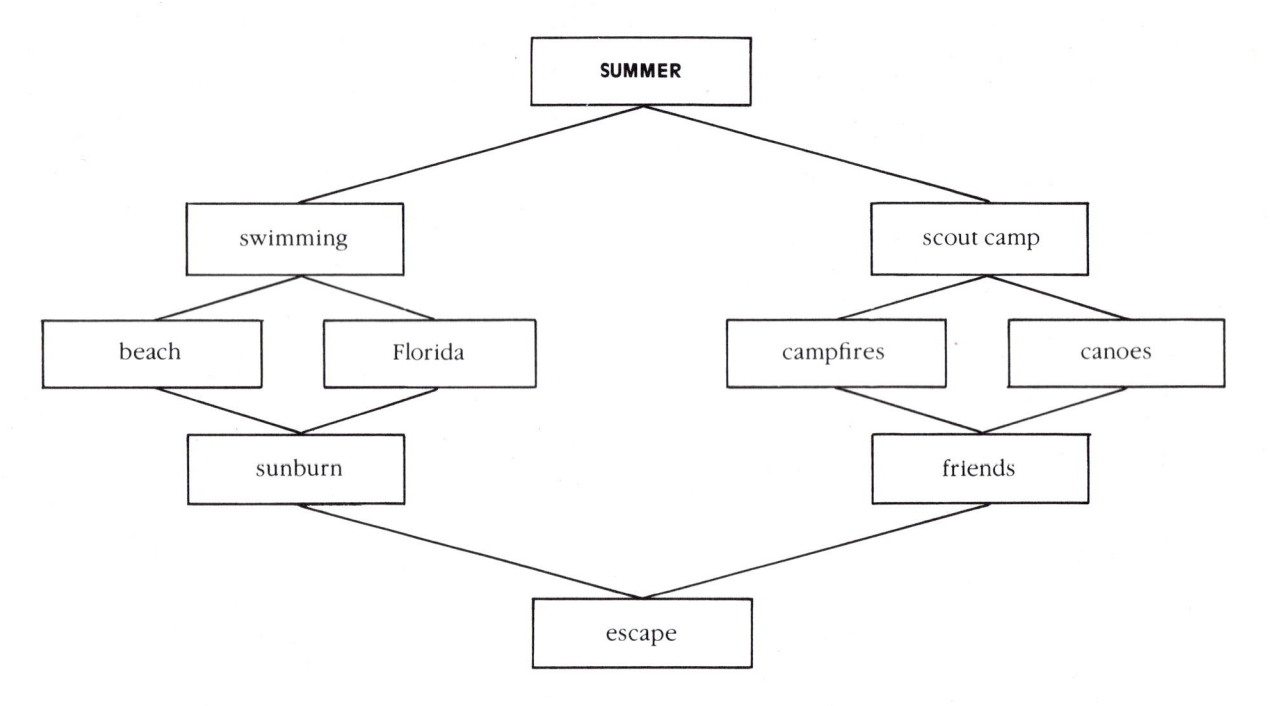

```
                    SUMMER
                   /      \
            swimming      scout camp
            /    \         /      \
         beach   Florida  campfires  canoes
            \    /              \    /
           sunburn              friends
                \              /
                  \          /
                    escape
```

Notice how the word *summer* triggers experiences and feelings that lead in two directions—scout camp and swimming. Swimming then branches into its own cluster of associations. So does scout camp. The bottom box brings together all the associations. Both swimming and scout camp suggest escape. Maybe that's what summer is all about.

ON YOUR OWN

These boxes and lines are a kind of map of how a mind works. Try this yourself with a mind map. On a piece of paper, trace the diagram below. Then fill it in with words you associate with *school*.

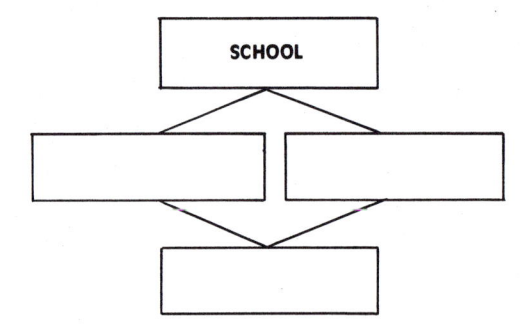

```
        SCHOOL
        /    \
      [  ]  [  ]
        \    /
         [  ]
```

18 Unit I

How are the first and last words in your map related?

Now try a more complicated map. Look back at the summer map on page 18. Notice the pattern. The "sunburn" box has the idea "sunburn," which is common to both "beach" and "Florida" above it; the "friends" box has the idea "friends," which is common to the ideas "campfires" and "canoes." Trace the diagram below, and follow that pattern in your boxes for the birthday map.

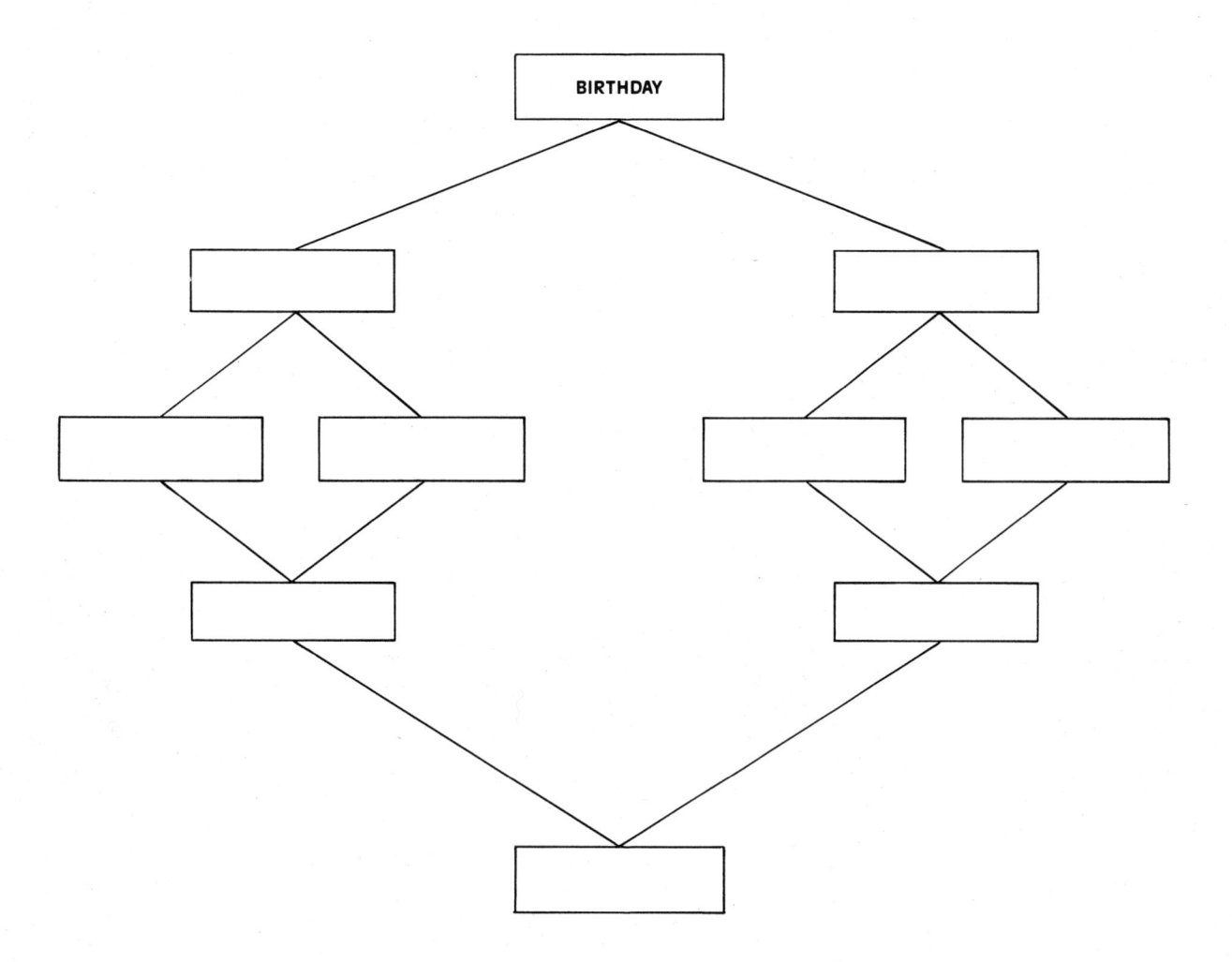

Save your birthday map in your portfolio or sketchbook. You'll need it later. Now, the important thing is to understand how maps help us to see how our own minds work. Often, they work by association. When we hear a special song or smell a favorite food or see a familiar object, associations crowd our minds. Associating is an important way of thinking.

Experiencing the Arts 19

ACTIVITY

Maps into Poems

Poets are people who put words together in special ways. They "see" something, and then create a word picture so that others can see it too. Look back at the summer map on page 18. Could there be a poem in there somewhere?

SUMMER

swimming and scout camp
sunburned Florida beaches
friendly campfires and canoes
happy escapes

See how easily the words become lines in a poem?

ON YOUR OWN

In your sketchbook experiment with ways to shape your birthday map into a poem. Add some words if you need to. Arrange the words in your poem so that they sound good to you. Read your poem to a friend.

Going Beyond

Try mapping other words. Try "friends" or "family" or "Christmas" or "grandmother" or "disasters." See what kinds of associations present themselves. Try turning several of your maps into poems.

Tuning in on Sounds

Until now, you've been trying to "see" more. As you were writing your poem, though, you probably found yourself working with sound and meaning too. That's good. The way a poem sounds is important. Poems are read with the ears as well as with the eyes.

That's how you'll want to read Eve Merriam's poem about a rusty water spigot. This poem is a good example of how words can recreate sounds.

> The rusty spigot
> sputters,
> utters
> a splutter,
> spatters a smattering of drops,
> gashes wider;
> slash,
> splatters,
> scatters,
> spurts,
> finally stops sputtering
> and plash!
> gushes rushes splashes
> clear water dashes.

The person who wrote this poem had not just looked at rusty spigots. She had listened to them.

Poets are good listeners. They don't let sounds pass unnoticed. With a little practice, you too can tune in on the rich world of sound that surrounds all of us.

ACTIVITY

Sounds of School

ON YOUR OWN

To get started, you need not leave your classroom. Just sit quietly and listen. In your sketchbook, list every sound you can hear no matter how slight. Spend at least five minutes logging everything you hear.

Experiencing the Arts

AS A CLASS

Share your sound log with the rest of the class. As your teacher or a classmate compiles a list on the board, check for sounds you missed. Which sounds did almost everyone hear? Which ones did only a few people hear? Take a moment to think about why people might have heard different sounds.

ACTIVITY

Searching Out Sounds

ON YOUR OWN

Take your sketchbook to some place that buzzes with sound—perhaps the school cafeteria during lunch, the gym or stadium during practice or a game, a video arcade, a laundromat, or a busy shopping mall. Spend ten minutes listening for sounds and listing them.

IN A GROUP

In class, share your sound log with a small group. Mention a particular sound and see if the group can guess where you heard it. After comparing lists, sort the sounds heard by members of your group into columns. Label the columns with such words as Loud, Soft, Short, High, Low, Angry, Impatient, Happy, Hurt, Excited. Choose your own categories. Be sure that each sound fits into at least one category. Don't worry if some fit into two or more.

On a large sheet of paper or on the chalkboard, make a chart showing how your group sorted the sounds. Compare your chart with those done by other groups.

Going Beyond

Select a place that sounds different at different times of the day or week. Make two sound logs and compare them.

Tape a sound collage—a sequence of sounds that form a pattern or tell a story—and play it for the class.

Make lists with such titles as Summer Sounds, Winter Sounds, Wake-up Sounds, City Sounds, Halloween Sounds, or Sounds I Never Want to Hear. Shape one of your collections into a sound poem. (A sound poem is a list of sounds arranged into poetic lines.)

ACTIVITY

Tuning in to Music

ON YOUR OWN

Listen as your teacher plays a recording or as you play one on your own. Try to block out everything else and concentrate on the music. If the song has words, ignore them.

Think about what you heard and how you responded. Did the music move fast or slow? Was it smooth or jerky? Heavy or light? Did it seem different at the beginning, middle, and end? In your sketchbook, draw lines to show how the music moved.

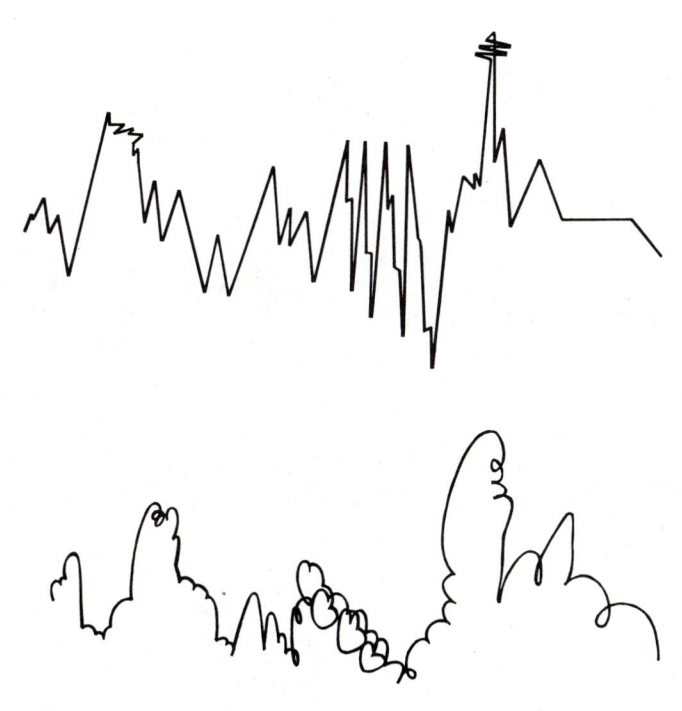

Listen to the recording again. This time, see how many different instruments you can hear. List the instruments. Then try some associating as you did with colors. What does the music make you think of? What color do you associate with the sound of each instrument? What shape?

IN A GROUP

Share your music line with three or four classmates. How are the music lines the same? How are they different? Also share your list of instruments and associations. Did any instrument suggest the same color or shape to several members of the group? Where were the greatest differences?

Experiencing the Arts 23

ACTIVITY

Making Your Own Music

Music is sound, but not all sound is music. During this activity, you will try your hand at turning sounds into music.

Think how many different sounds you can make with ordinary objects. For example, you can jingle keys, rub two pieces of sandpaper together, tap a spoon against glasses holding different amounts of water. You can also make sound with your own body by shuffling feet, clapping hands, and snapping fingers.

> IN A GROUP

Working with a small group of classmates, list ways to make interesting sounds with ordinary things. Make your list as long as you can. Decide on several sound-makers to use in composing your own music.

Begin by experimenting with various sounds. Try repeating, alternating, and combining different pitches (high and low notes). Try different rhythms. Keep going until the group finds a pattern everyone likes.

ACTIVITY

Scoring the Composition

> IN A GROUP

Earlier in this unit you arranged the objects you found to form a visual statement. You have also arranged words to create a poem. In this activity you will arrange sounds to create a musical composition with a particular feeling.

Musical compositions are written as notes on something musicians call a "score." A musical score is a series of notes and symbols which tell musicians what to play and how to play it. It is a kind of map for them to follow. Look at the score on the facing page. It is from Tchaikovsky's *Sleeping Beauty*.

The notes tell the musician the pitch and the pace of the music. Other symbols suggest the volume (loud or soft) and the emotional quality the composer wants to create (intense, calm, frantic).

As amateur musicians with a couple of wooden spoons, a glass, a piece of sandpaper, or some other simple instruments, your ensemble will not need a sophisticated musical score like Beethoven or Mozart. You will need some organized way of performing your sounds, however. You and your fellow musicians can create a simple score or plan by experimenting with sounds you can make together. Work to create sounds that communicate a particular feeling: joy, sorrow, surprise, anger. Use the rhythm and pitch of your sounds to help capture the feeling you want. Once you have experimented with sounds, you are ready to write a score.

Here are some ways to write your score:

- You might simply list the initials of your band members, and then write these initials on paper to show when members should make their sounds. If, for example, your names are Ken, Mindy, Ray, and Juan, your score might look like this:

K, K, J—K, K, J—R, M, R, M—K, K, J—R, J, R, J—MMMMMM

Experiencing the Arts 25

The letters indicate when each member plays; the dashes indicate pauses. If you need more directions like loud and soft, add those. If you need any other dramatics, add them.

- Another option, if someone in your group reads music, is to use real notes indicating when high sounds are played and low sounds are played.

- Other options include assigning each member of the group a shape (circle, triangle, square, etc.) and then indicating sounds by placing shapes on your score.

You may devise any system you choose to score your composition. The most important point is that all members of your ensemble be able to see the score and perform it with precision. Once you have a score, you are ready to practice your composition and prepare to perform it for classmates. You may find it much easier to perform your composition if you appoint someone to lead the group. A director can help keep everyone together and add a professional touch to your work.

Print a copy of your final score on a large piece of paper so classmates can see it while you are performing. Your teacher may ask you to explain your system after the performance.

ON YOUR OWN

In your sketchbook respond to these questions:

1. What title would you suggest for your group's composition? Why?
2. To you, what was the easiest part of making and scoring your own composition? What part was hardest?
3. In what ways is arranging sounds into music like arranging objects into a tabletop composition? Like arranging words into a poem? Which activity did you like best?

Place a copy of your group's musical score in your portfolio and save it for future reference.

Performing the Poem

Throughout this unit you've worn a variety of creators' hats: you've been an artist, a poet, and a composer. These creators often do much of their work alone and in private. They are guided by their own personal visions.

Musicians, dancers, and actors are also artists, but they work differently. Musicians follow a composer's score and are led by a conductor. Dancers follow music and are directed by a choreographer. Actors read their lines from a script and are coached by a director. We call these artists "performers" because they create their art in front of groups. Artists, composers, and poets can work alone, in private places, but performers must share their work on stage. Your next artistic challenge will be to perform something composed by someone else—a poem.

ACTIVITY

Seeing a Poem

AS A CLASS

Using images, poems bring pictures to our minds as we read them. Close your eyes and relax. Listen and see what pictures come to mind as your teacher reads this poem to you:

ABSOLUTES
(From an ink painting by Seiho)

black on white
crow in snow
   hunched
   wet lump
on brittle branch
remembering warmth
remembering corn
miserable
as life
is
black on white

   Gustave Keyser

Experiencing the Arts

What pictures did you see while you listened to the poet's words? Was there one very strong picture or were there several rather fuzzy ones? Close your eyes again. Is the picture still there? If you were going to share this poem with someone and you couldn't use words, how would you do it? Could you draw a picture or act it out?

ACTIVITY

Seeing More Poems

ON YOUR OWN

Here are three poems to read and respond to. Have your sketchbook ready. Read each poem; then jot down the strongest pictures from the poem. If each poem were going to be a movie, what would the camera see?

ENDING

The sky is falling;
Blue pieces lie among the daisies.
If I pick one up
And hold it to my eye
The world is simple.

Stars sparkle in the grass.
I'll twist one
In my hair, and
Run barefoot through
The scattered sky.

When the sun plummets down
Catch it for a yellow ball.
We'll arc it high
Where the sky once was.

Lyra Ward
Student
Detroit, Michigan

IN-TRADE

Andrea always
Liked to share
So
When she died
We felt no guilt
At taking the flowers off her grave
And selling them door to door
Until we had
Enough to buy
A fuzzy cocker pup.

Lola Sierra
Student
Sierra Madre, California

TO SATCH
(Satchel Paige was a famous baseball pitcher.)

Sometimes I feel like I will *never* stop
Just go on forever
Til one fine mornin'

I'm gonna reach up and grab me a handfulla stars
Swing out my long lean leg
And whip three hot strikes burnin' down the heavens
And look over at God and say
How about that!

Samuel Allen

IN A GROUP

Select your favorite poem of the three. Then form a group with four or five others who chose the same poem. In your group, accomplish the following things:

- Explain why this is your favorite of the three poems.
- Share notes from your sketchbook about the pictures this poem provokes.

Experiencing the Arts

- Decide on a way to "perform" this poem for the class. Consider these options:

    Several students may act out the poem while someone reads it.

    You may do a choral reading with different students reading different lines.

    You may "freeze" a picture from the poem by creating a living sculpture while someone reads the poem.

    You may decide to do some free-form movement, much like dance, while someone reads the poem.

    You may do almost anything else you can think of to perform the poem for your classmates.

  Practice your performance and then present it before the class.

Celebrating Success

You started this unit with an empty portfolio and a blank sketchbook. Now, both should hold a satisfying collection of your own drawings, writings, and other creations. Some are probably near misses. Others have potential but need a lot more work. Then there are a few pieces you're really proud of, as you probably are of some of your performances. That kind of success is worth celebrating. You'll do so by holding a class art festival.

ACTIVITY

Preparing for the Art Festival

> **ON YOUR OWN**

The first step in preparing for the festival is to decide on your own individual entry. See what's in your portfolio and your sketchbook. Also consider creations that wouldn't fit into either one—creations like sound tapes and three-dimensional pieces. Choose a favorite to display or perform at the festival. Jot down the title and the category—for example, drawing, poem, sound collage.

You may decide that your creation is ready to go public just as it is. You may decide that it needs more work. If so, it might be best to work on it at home as you spend class time organizing the festival.

> **AS A CLASS**

A good art festival takes careful planning. After setting a date for your class festival, start that planning with two chalkboard charts, one for displays and one for performances.

DISPLAYS

Name	Title	Category

PERFORMANCES

Name	Title	Category

Give a recorder the information needed to list your entry on the appropriate chart.

After all festival entries have been listed, help the recorder make another chalkboard list, this time by category. Under DISPLAYS, for example, you should list all paintings together, all poems together, and so on. This listing by category will tell you what entries go together at the festival. It will also help you decide how much space will be needed for each kind of display and how much time will be needed for each kind of performance. Copy these lists from the chalkboard for later use.

By now, you realize that a good festival doesn't just happen. It takes work. You'll probably find it most efficient to do most of that work in committees.

The first step in organizing committees is deciding what major jobs need to be done. Make a chalkboard list of possible jobs—for example, arranging display space, scheduling performances, making programs or placards, inviting special guests. Together, decide on four or five committees and who will serve on each.

Experiencing the Arts

IN A GROUP

Meet with your committee and select a chair. Then explore your particular task. Decide in detail what needs to be done and when. Decide also which committee members will take responsibility for each job. Help your committee chair summarize assignments on a chart like this:

Task	Member Responsible	Deadline Date

Ask your teacher to check over your chart. Then share it with the class and post it on a bulletin board designated by your teacher.

As you complete assigned tasks, report to your committee chair so that he or she can check off that task on the chart. This check-off system will help you monitor progress toward the big celebration.

Meanwhile, be sure that your own entry is ready to display or perform. It's *your* art that's being celebrated.

ACTIVITY

Art Festival

AS A CLASS

If your committees have functioned smoothly, your classroom should look a little like an art gallery by now. You probably have a special place for performances. You may even have special guests like the school principal and your parents. Now it's time to celebrate.

Enjoy the performances. Take time to look closely at each exhibit. Talk to other artists. Tell them what you like best. Ask questions about their work. You may even want to collect autographs in your sketchbook, or pretend that you are a judge and cast your own private vote for the best entry in each category and for best-of-show.

ACTIVITY

Looking Back

ON YOUR OWN

Now that the art festival is over and your classroom is beginning to look like a classroom again, take time to go back and reflect on what you've done in this unit. Reflect also on how you've done it. That's the way good thinkers learn how their own minds work.

Again, look back through your portfolio and your sketchbook. Look at your entry in the art festival. Try to remember what you thought and how you felt as you did each piece of work—the contour drawing, sensory tour notes, tabletop composition, birthday poem, sound log, musical score, and images from the poem you performed. Choose the activity you liked doing best, the one in which you became most deeply involved.

In your sketchbook, retrace that experience in writing. Tell as much as you can about the way you thought your way through the activity. You may also want to talk about what kind of thinking you do best. Try to focus on how your mind worked rather than on the steps you took.

Reading what Terri wrote in her sketchbook may help you get the idea:

October 15

I liked the sensory tour best. I just went outside by myself and opened my eyes and ears. I tried to "take in" everything. My mind was just sort of recording like a camera.

Then I brought my list to class and we made categories on the board. I saw what other people collected on their sensory tour, and my mind was thinking, "Oh, that's a good one." or "I should have seen that." So I guess I was comparing what I experienced with other kids. My mind was also putting things into categories.

Then when we made the tabletop composition, we just sort of put things together until they "looked right." I guess I had a picture in my mind of how that should look, and I kept changing things until it looked right.

It seems like this experience was mostly seeing things and arranging things.

I think my mind is pretty organized most of the time, and that's why I'm good at arranging things.

Remember, talk about how your mind was working while you were doing the activity.

Your teacher may ask you to share your reflection with a friend, a small group, or the whole class. Notice that different people thought through the same task in different ways. We can learn about thinking from hearing how other people think. The most important thing, though, is to learn how our own minds work.

Experiencing the Arts 33

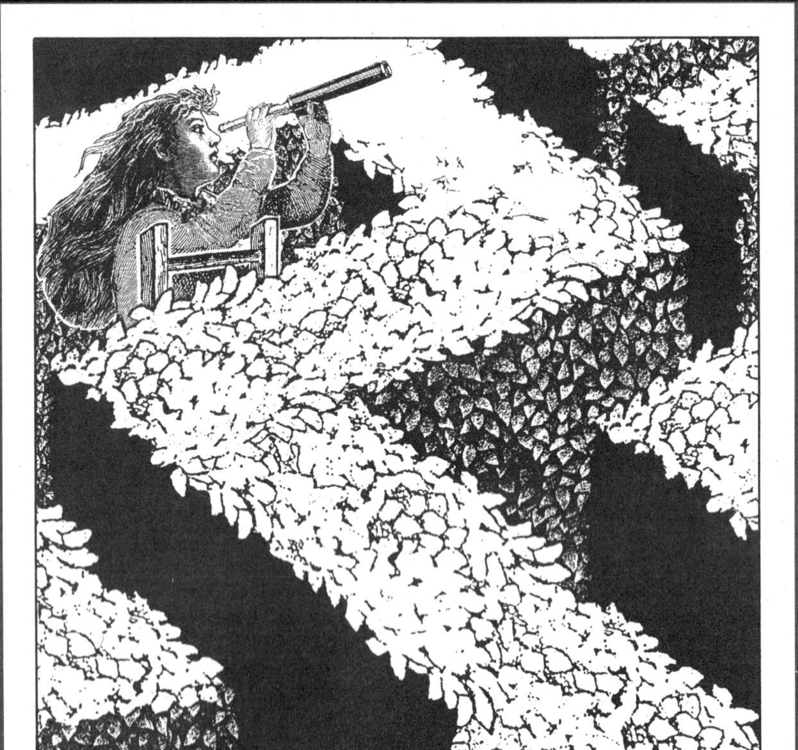

UNIT II Exploring Possibilities

N Unit I, you practiced thinking like an artist. You concentrated on "seeing" with your senses. In this unit, you'll practice thinking like an inventor. You'll try a special kind of seeing called *speculation*.

That means looking at things not as they are, but as they might be. It means guessing. Inventors do a lot of speculating about what might work.

Here is one inventor's idea for a new kind of bus that might work. It's called a Collective Responsibility Vehicle because the passengers drive it themselves.

The story of the Collective Responsibility Vehicle tells a lot about how inventors think. It also sets the stage for the kind of thinking you'll be doing in this unit.

Spotlight on the CRV

This particular inventor rode buses everywhere he went. One day he got to thinking about the inconvenience of waiting on large buses that don't run very often. He knew that more frequent smaller buses would be handier, but realized that hiring so many drivers would be expensive. In mulling over ways to save on labor costs, he remembered self-service gas stations, car washes, and supermarkets. He wondered why not let passengers drive the buses themselves. That idea inspired the CRV.

Every seat on this vehicle has its own steering wheel, control, and TV view of the road ahead. A central minicomputer scans the signals from each passenger's steering wheel, accelerator, and brake. It averages the signals and sends them to the wheels of the bus. The wheels move accordingly.

Of course, this kind of bus would not really work, although technology is certainly advanced enough to allow its production. The idea of such a bus just does not make sense.

Inventor at Work

Right now, the point is not whether the CRV will ever make it off the drawing board. The point is what went into inventing it. First, the inventor saw a problem. In rummaging through his mind for ways to solve it, he recalled how gas stations and supermarkets had solved similar problems. These connections led to the idea of a self-service bus. The idea seemed worth exploring, especially since the inventor knew enough about the engineering of large vehicles, minicomputers, and television to see some exciting possibilities. Of course, he had to find out more. He also had to do some complicated planning to put all the parts together into a workable system. Planning was often trial-and-error. The inventor had to keep looking at his design with a critical eye, making changes as he went along. Still, his idea didn't work.

You can see that invention is no simple matter. Inventors are problem-finders and problem-solvers. They do lots of imagining, comparing, connecting, investigating, planning, and evaluating. These kinds of thinking are a big part of everyday life—in school and out. That's why it's worth your while to practice thinking like an inventor.

ACTIVITY

Inventor's Notebook

A notebook is to an inventor what a sketchbook is to an artist. It's a place to collect ideas, then follow them and see where they lead. You'll soon investigate further how inventors find and follow ideas. Before you begin, though, you'll need your own place to think on paper.

ON YOUR OWN

Have an inventor's notebook handy. It can be as simple as a spiral notebook or a folder with plenty of paper held in place.

In any case, make your notebook look like it belongs to an inventor. One possibility is to cover it with pictures of your own favorite inventions—for example, the telephone, TV, a certain car, blue jeans, super glue. You'll think of other possibilities.

Pushing the Limits

Let's return to that earlier example (page 37) about whether a Collective Responsibility Vehicle really makes sense. In that case, the idea was outrageous, but so were some other ideas when they were first proposed. "Experts" laughed at the Wright brothers' Kitty Hawk experiment, predicted that television would never get beyond a few demonstration models, and scoffed at the idea that human beings would ever set foot on the moon. Before writing off the self-service bus—or any other invention—as nonsense, consider this statement by a respected scientist: "A novel idea always looks crazy. Of course, it can be wrong-crazy. The interesting situation is when the idea is crazy but right."

Inventors use their imaginations to push the limits of possibility. Imagining may be the most important thing an inventor does. The first major question about inventing is where ideas come from in the first place. In exploring this question, you'll give your own imagination a workout.

ACTIVITY

Second-Guessing Inventors

ON YOUR OWN

Take a few minutes to imagine how some familiar devices might have been invented. Consider the following:

- the waffle iron
- the personal headphone stereo
- the bicycle
- the typewriter
- the lawnmower
- the waterbed
- the helicopter
- the vacuum cleaner
- the popcorn popper
- the parachute

You may already have a little information about how one or two of these devices were invented. If not, make up some. How long has each device been around? What kind of person might have invented it? What problem might that person have been trying to solve? What might have triggered the idea for a particular invention?

Choose the three inventions that interest you most. Turn your imagination loose and think of a story that explains how each of the three devices came to be invented. Jot down your basic ideas before they get away.

WITH A PARTNER

Tell all three stories to a partner. Ask each other questions and comment on details you like best. With the help of your partner, decide which of your three stories would be most interesting to read and the most fun to write. Jot down highlights to use in writing that story.

ON YOUR OWN

Think of a good way to write out your story—maybe as a first-person account by the inventor, as a talk-show interview, or as imagined pages from the inventor's notebook. Write in any form you wish, but

Exploring Possibilities 39

show the inventor's mind in action. Show how the inventor might have found ideas and followed up on them.

Claudette's story may help you get started. Make your story about as long as hers.

Scene: the kitchen of Waffleshire Castle in England
Time: the present
Speaker: a tour guide

Here is the very room that made this castle so famous way back in the Middle Ages. It all started in this kitchen when Sir Reginald returned from the Crusades, all exhausted and hungry. He was wearing his heavy armor and barely able to struggle over to that bench before he collapsed. He didn't even notice that he was collapsing on a neat row of dough cakes his wife had set there to cool.

She noticed. "How could you, Reginald? Look what that armor of yours has done to my cakes. Now they are all crinkled."

"Sorry, Fiona, my love. I'll eat them anyway. Just get me some butter and honey."

That's how the story goes in Sir Reginald's diary. The next page tells about eating the cakes. Even Lady Fiona liked the way butter and honey settled into the low places. Keeping honey on the cakes had always been a problem.

Sir Reginald knew he was on to something. Yet it seemed like an awful lot of trouble to put on heavy armor every time he wanted what he now called a waffle.

He thought and thought. Maybe he could cut his armor up into cake-sized pieces. After all, the Crusades were over. But by themselves those pieces wouldn't be heavy enough to crimp the cakes.

He cut up his armor anyway, placed a piece on each warm cake his wife had made, and sat down on them one by one. Still too much trouble!

Then he thought, "Why bake the cakes and then crimp them? Maybe there's a way to crimp them while they bake."

The next morning he got one of Fiona's cake pans, the iron kind with a long handle for holding over coals in the fireplace. He put a piece of armor in the bottom of the pan.

"Fiona," he called. "Come try out this iron pan for waffles."

Of course, it worked and the name was later shortened to waffle iron.

Just thinks, folks, it happened right here.

Claudette had once heard someone say that waffles were invented when a knight in armor sat down on a cake. She had no idea how accurate this information was, but she let her imagination play with it. That's how she came up with her story.

With or without information, you can do the same thing. Use any ideas you jotted down earlier. Let your imagination play. Try to think like your fictitious inventor. Make your story the first entry in your inventor's notebook.

IN A GROUP

Share your story of an invention with four or five classmates. Talk about the parts of each story you like best, the parts that seem most imaginative. Then talk about the stories as studies in how inventors' minds work. Do any of the inventors in the stories show open-mindedness? Willingness to take risks? Playfulness? Real inventors seem to share these characteristics. They make mental leaps and follow unlikely hunches. Sometimes, they start looking for one thing and find something better. Such lucky accidents wouldn't happen if inventors weren't open to all kinds of possibilities. Openness is part of imagination.

Do any of the inventors in the stories show persistence? Successful inventors back up imagination with hard work. They don't give up. It took Thomas Edison thirteen years to build his first crude model of the phonograph. During these years, he used his hands to try out ideas that began in his head.

Looking Ahead

You've already loosened up your imagination by writing a story and by brainstorming. Now, you'll concentrate on examining new technologies. This will lead to a Technology Display, prepared by teams of students. With a background in technology you'll go on to do the kind of inventing scientists do. Like Edison, you'll use your hands to try out ideas that begin in your head. Your individual invention will be your exhibit in an inventors' fair presented by your class at the end of the unit.

New Technologies

As an inventor of the 1980s, you have tools that previously existed only in science fiction. You have technology at your fingertips. Consider the classic example of trying to build a better mousetrap. Today's better mousetrap—actually a mouse repellent—is ultrasonic, that is, controlled by sound waves. So are new diagnostic techniques in medicine. Ultrasound is also used by geologists to "see"

Exploring Possibilities 41

underground and by jewelers, scientists, and manufacturers to scrub surfaces that must be extra clean. Ultrasonics is a major technology—an advanced science with all kinds of applications. It is also a powerful tool for inventors.

Just in the 1980s, there have been two new technologies that will change entertainment in the home—video cassette recorders and compact disc recording. The first will enable you to reproduce television programs, and the second will produce better stereo sound without the use of the now old-fashioned phonograph needle.

ACTIVITY

Ranking Technologies

ON YOUR OWN

A technology is an application of science that achieves a desired end, such as drilling for oil, communicating over long distances, or diagnosing illnesses. Look at the inventions illustrated and name the technologies they represent. What are some major technologies not represented? In your inventor's notebook, jot down the ones you expect to change life most dramatically during the next twenty-five years. Rank those technologies according to potential influence on the future.

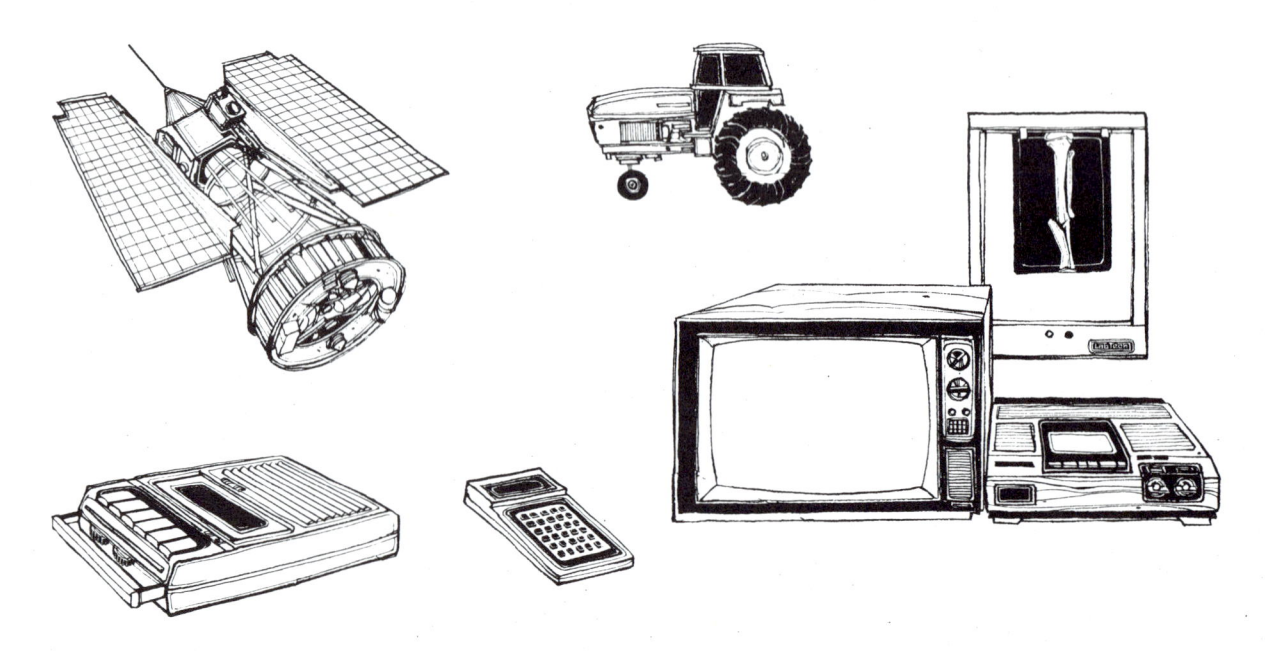

AS A CLASS

"Vote" for your top three technologies as a recorder tallies votes on the chalkboard. Help count votes and make a class survey. Copy the list in your inventor's notebook. How close are the class rankings to your own?

Talk about the technologies on the class list. Justify each choice. Give examples of the changes you expect each technology to bring about.

Going Beyond

Look around you for evidence of technology at work and complete at least one of these activities. Record results in your inventor's notebook.

- Do a technology survey of your own home or school. List several applications of technology you can find.

- Go through three issues of your local newspaper. Clip all articles that mention one of the major technologies.

- Over several days of viewing, keep a log of TV references to technology. Include newscasts as well as action shows like hospital and police dramas. Look as well as listen for examples.

- Interview an adult whose work involves technology. Find out what jobs technology does and how.

ACTIVITY

Taking Stock

ON YOUR OWN

Review your class list of technologies. Even though you may still be working on your "Going Beyond" project, review any information you may have collected in your inventor's notebook.

Exploring Possibilities 43

How many of these technologies do you find?

- Computers
- Lasers
- Video
- Robotics
- Satellites

Which one of the five do you know most about? Right now, which interests you most?

IN A GROUP

Join a small group of classmates interested in the same technology. Using entries in your inventor's notebook and anything else you can remember, pool information about that technology. Piece that information together. Ask one group member to summarize in writing.

Look for gaps in what you know. What don't you understand about the technology itself? What do you need to know more about? Make a list of questions that you would need to explore if you decided to work with this technology.

Where would you find this information? You probably know some technology experts in your own school and community. Who are they? Is there a nearby science museum that features exhibits and programs on your technology? Where would you look for such information in your school and public library? In what magazines? Make a list of these sources.

As a group, prepare a basic explanation of your technology for the rest of the class. Use an interesting format—for example, a panel discussion or a press conference. Keep your explanations simple and use lots of examples. Avoid technical terms that some of your classmates may not know.

AS A CLASS

Listen closely to the explanations from other groups. Think about the future possibilities of each technology. Follow-up discussions will give you a chance to ask questions and add information.

After the presentations, think about what you've learned. Now that you know more about several technologies, which interests you most? That is the technology you'll describe with a team of your classmates in the Technology Display.

ACTIVITY

Organizing to Find Information

AS A GROUP

Form a team with several students who chose the same technology you did. Since your technology team will be working together for a while, you may want to give yourselves a name. Choose a name that identifies your technology—for example, Sci-Fi or Satellites. Then design a team logo based on your name. Here are two other groups' logos to help you get the idea:

Make a large poster with your logo at the top. Below, list members of the team. Put your poster aside to use later.

Your team's main task is finding information. You'll do a better job if you take a little time to get organized. Plan to investigate the first two questions about your technology:

- How does it work?
- What are the different uses of the technology?

Decide on a way of compiling information as it is collected. For example, you might start a card file for each question. Working individually, you could jot down new information on cards or slips of paper. After sharing the information with the team, you could file your notes under the appropriate question.

After your team decides on a system, try it out by organizing the information you already have. Work in small subcommittees to summarize what you know about how the technology works, how it is used today, and how it might be used tomorrow. Discuss those summaries and file them for reference.

Decide how you'll work as a research team. Should you tackle the two questions one at a time? Should different people work on different questions? What are the advantages and disadvantages of slicing up the job?

You'll find it helpful to make a list of resources available to the team. Who knows a particular school or community expert? Who subscribes to a technical magazine? Who knows how to use the library?

Exploring Possibilities

Team members might volunteer to tap resources they know best.

In any case, individual team members will need to record their findings carefully. These findings will be shared at meetings. Plan to meet often. Research is not a one-shot job. You'll continue to stockpile information even as you put the finishing touches on your own invention.

Since technologies overlap so much, you may even get some help from friends on other teams. Set up a collection center to encourage such contributions. If possible, attach your team poster to a section of the classroom wall designated by your teacher. Nearby, provide a box or a large envelope to hold information contributed by other teams. Save the description of your technology for when you rejoin your technology group.

Going Beyond

As you research your own technology, be on the alert for information about those being researched by other teams. Jot down anything you happen to find. Leave your notes at the appropriate collection center.

ACTIVITY

The Technology Display

AS A GROUP

With the other members of your technology team, plan and assemble a large wall chart which will introduce your technology to nonexperts. The chart should be neatly lettered and easily readable from four to six feet away. Be sure your chart displays these things clearly:

1. The name of the technology in large letters. Drawings or pictures cut from magazines would add to the appeal of your chart.

2. A "How It Works" section. This section should have a brief but complete explanation of how your technology works. Avoid highly technical language, and define any technical terms you do use. Use pictures and diagrams if you need to.

3. A "Contemporary Applications" section. This section should be a list of places where your technology is already in use. Be specific. Just listing "medicine," for example, would be too general. List some specific applications in medicine: eye surgery, brain scans, and so on.

4. A "Future Applications" section. This is another list of where your technology may be applied in the future. Make some guesses here if you like. Speculate a little about the possibilities offered by your invention.

5. Finally, your chart should display the name of your team, the logo, and the names of individual team members.

Brainstorming Alternatives for Individual Inventions

Now that you have learned a lot about technologies, you are ready to consider an invention.

Inventors work with information and with tools. Most of all, though, they work with ideas. That's where imagination comes in. Like all creative people, inventors work from an abundance of ideas. As you have already discovered, they stay open to every possibility, no matter how strange it may seem. They go first for quantity and then for quality.

One technique for such creative thinking is called *brainstorming*. Actually, you've already done some team brainstorming. Remember back in Unit I when you and several others listed ways to make sounds with ordinary objects? You tried for the longest list you could make. You kept the ideas flowing as long as you could. That was brainstorming. This time, the whole class will work together. Your task will be to generate as many ideas as possible as fast as possible. Observe these simple rules:

1. Let the ideas flow and call them out fast.
2. Suspend judgment—no criticism allowed.
3. Record all ideas.
4. Piggyback on others' ideas—that is, take those ideas further or in a different direction.

Good brainstorming is fast and freewheeling. Even so, it's important to talk one at a time. Also, you'll need more than one recorder to capture all the ideas. Recorders can alternate writing down the ideas being called out. They may write with marking pens on paper taped to the wall or on the chalkboard. The important thing is to record every idea suggested without interrupting the flow. Push yourself to keep that flow going. If you get stuck, take off from a previous idea. Go beyond the obvious. Don't hesitate to be outrageous.

ACTIVITY

Brainstorming Warm-Up

AS A CLASS

Ready? Here's your first practice exercise. Brainstorm a list of disposables—things that are ordinarily thrown away. Include items that are discarded at home, at school, at factories, and in places of business. Include large things and small things. See how long a list the class can brainstorm.

IN A GROUP

Now try some small-group brainstorming. Choose two recorders to alternate. Select one disposable item from the list the class brainstormed. Suggest as many new uses for that item as you can. Remember, practicality doesn't count right now. Originality and quantity do. When you have finished, share your group list with the class.

Brainstorming Changes

Now that you've had some practice, you're ready to use brainstorming in laying more groundwork for an invention. You should be ready for the inventor's real question—what uses might be possible in the future?

Here are five areas where any new technology—including yours—might be applied:

- Home
- Recreation
- Transportation
- School
- Work

Which area of application interests you most? Form a group with others who chose the same area.

ACTIVITY

Brainstorming—Past, Present, and Future

IN A GROUP

Begin by brainstorming some history. If your group is interested in the home, think about how dwellings have changed since human beings first found shelter in caves, or how heating and cooling homes is different now.

If your group is interested in recreation, you might brainstorm the development of plays or musical instruments. Be sure to choose a brainstorming topic that members of your group know a little about. Don't make your topic too narrow, or you're likely to hit a dead end.

Once you have a topic, brainstorm as many kinds of homes, schools, recreation, work, or transportation as possible. Think about your topic over time, but don't worry too much about exact order. You can rearrange later. Go right up to the present. Make your list as long as possible.

Use your list to make a time line. Suppose, for example, that your group had brainstormed the history of musical instruments. If you had a rich list, it wouldn't be hard to construct a time line something like this:

NATURAL OBJECTS	SIMPLE CRAFTED INSTRUMENTS	MECHANICAL INSTRUMENTS	ELECTRONIC SOUND SIMULATORS
Animal horns	Flutes	Pianos	Miniature keyboards
Sticks	Bells	Violins	Computers
Hollow logs	Drums	Organs	
	Harps	Clarinets and other woodwinds	

Now that you have the idea, make your own time line. Put it on posterboard to share with the rest of the class later.

So far, in this activity you've brainstormed *past* changes in homes, schools, recreation, work, or transportation. Now, imagine changes that could take place in the *future*. In brainstorming future developments, let out all stops. Unleash your imagination. List as many possibilities as you can. Take turns acting as recorder.

Present your time line to the class. Also share your list of future possibilities.

Exploring Possibilities

Going Beyond

For some solo practice in brainstorming alternatives, complete one or more of these activities:

- Brainstorm uses for one-of-a-kind things—odd socks or gloves, a single earring or cufflink, one shoe.
- Make an inkblot. Study its shape and list ten things it could represent.
- Jot down the title of the last movie you saw or the last novel you read. List five other titles that would have been just as good.
- Clip several cartoons. Compose three new captions for each.

Focusing Problems

You've just done some brainstorming, letting your mind roam freely, picking up ideas from anywhere. When brainstorming goes well, you have an abundance of ideas. To be an effective problem-solver, such as a successful inventor, however, you need to narrow down a problem so that you can offer a creative solution.

Creative thinking is not necessarily messy or chaotic. Inventors sometimes work in systematic ways to find solutions. In the next activity, you will practice a technique for focusing your brainstorming so that your ideas lead down an orderly path.

ACTIVITY
Thinking Trees

ON YOUR OWN

Let's say that you are interested in inventing something to improve transportation. "Transportation" is a huge subject, and you could end up just spinning your wheels. One way to organize your thinking is to take a large idea like transportation and subdivide it into small units. For example, what kinds of transportation are there?

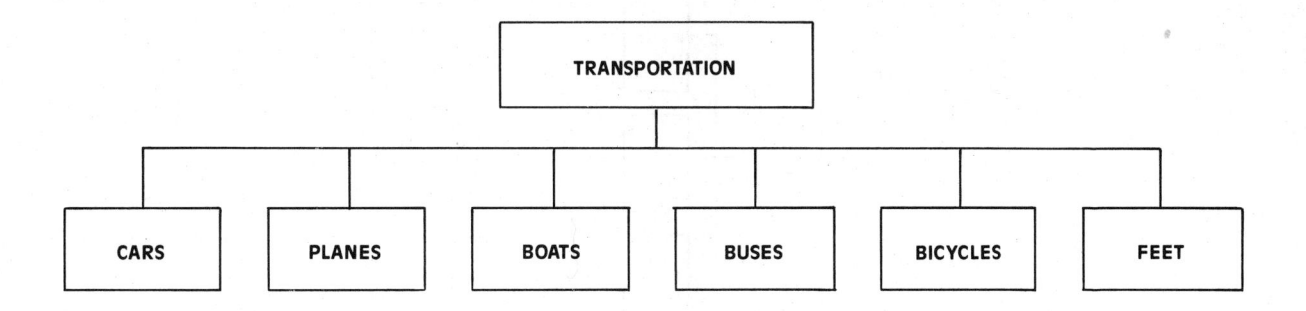

```
                    ┌──────────────────┐
                    │  TRANSPORTATION  │
                    └──────────────────┘
     ┌────────┬─────────┬─────────┼─────────┬──────────┐
  ┌──────┐ ┌──────┐ ┌──────┐ ┌──────┐ ┌────────┐ ┌──────┐
  │ CARS │ │PLANES│ │BOATS │ │BUSES │ │BICYCLES│ │ FEET │
  └──────┘ └──────┘ └──────┘ └──────┘ └────────┘ └──────┘
```

Can you think of other kinds of transportation?

Now what kinds of problems are associated with cars? Can you think of other problems?

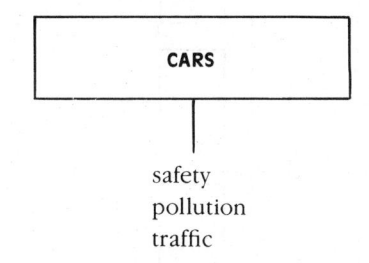

```
            ┌──────┐
            │ CARS │
            └──────┘
               │
            safety
            pollution
            traffic
```

Now we're going to subdivide each problem associated with cars. Think about what kinds of solutions or inventions already exist to solve these problems. Make each problem the heading for a list. We've started the lists for you.

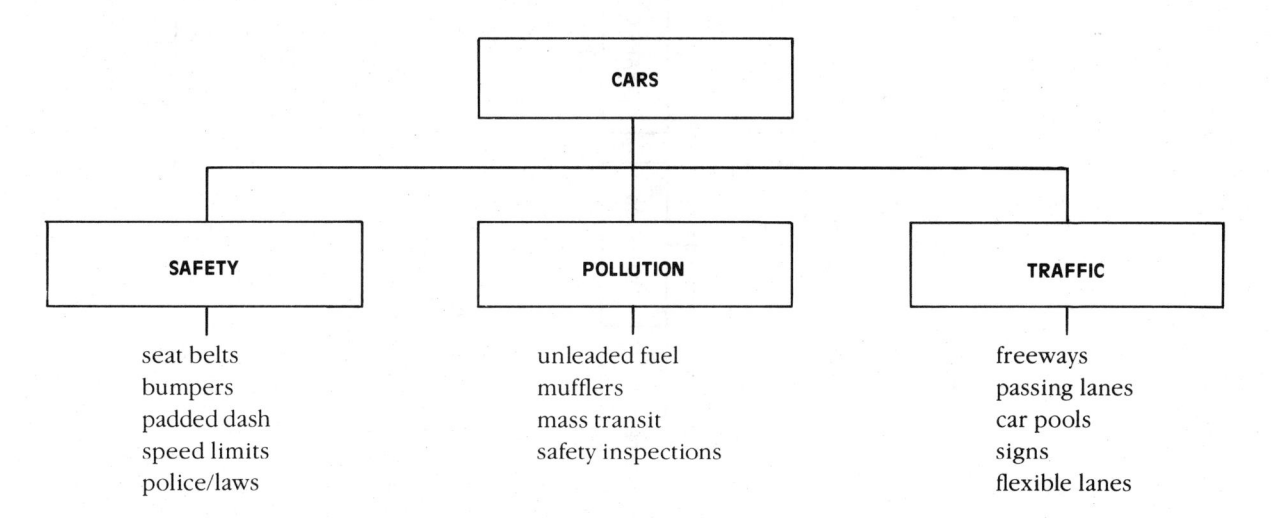

```
                    ┌──────┐
                    │ CARS │
                    └──────┘
        ┌──────────────┼──────────────┐
   ┌────────┐    ┌──────────┐    ┌────────┐
   │ SAFETY │    │ POLLUTION│    │ TRAFFIC│
   └────────┘    └──────────┘    └────────┘
```

SAFETY	POLLUTION	TRAFFIC
seat belts	unleaded fuel	freeways
bumpers	mufflers	passing lanes
padded dash	mass transit	car pools
speed limits	safety inspections	signs
police/laws		flexible lanes

Can you list more in each category?

Exploring Possibilities

TRANSPORTATION

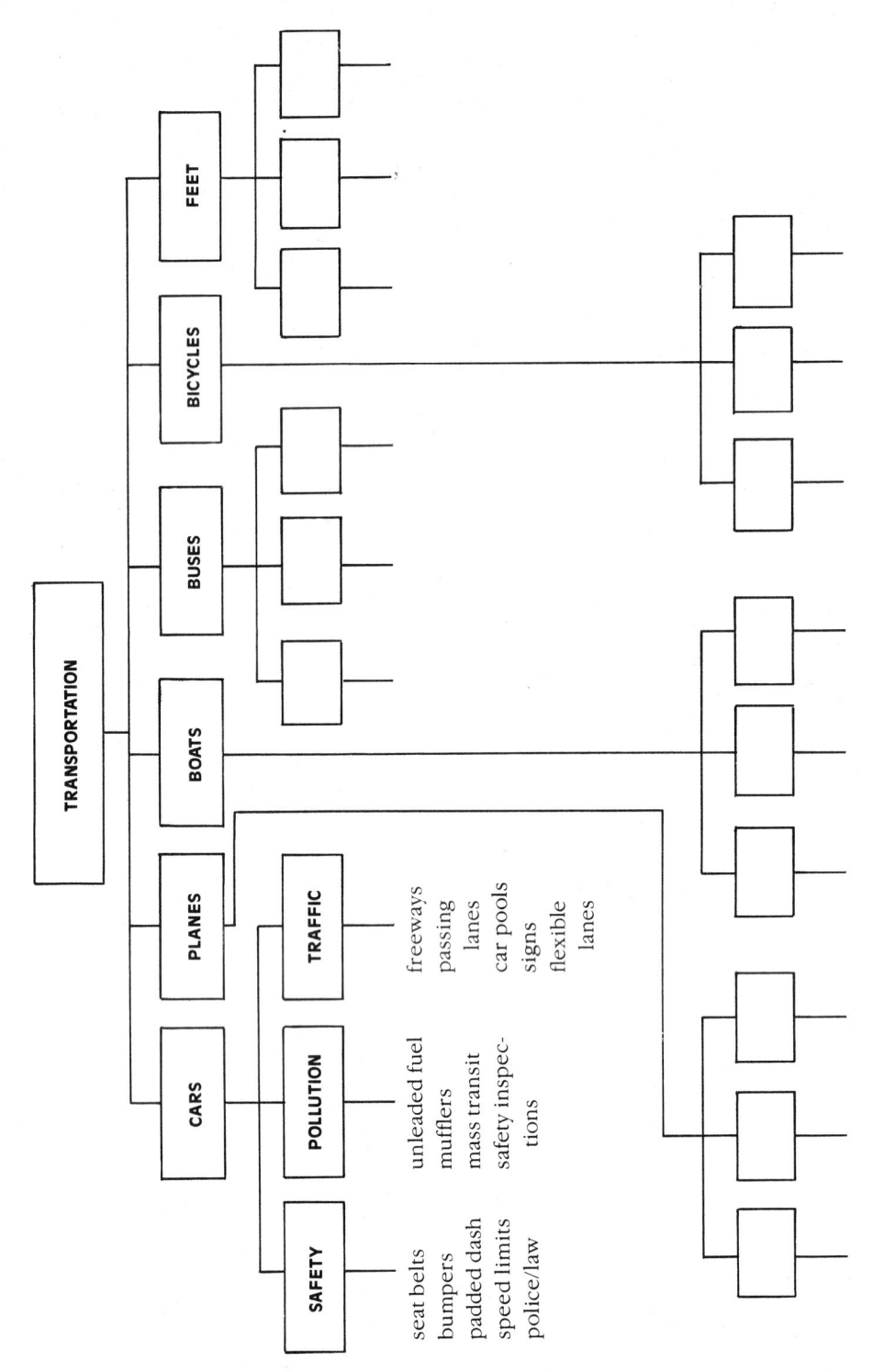

- PLANES
- CARS
  - SAFETY
    - seat belts
    - bumpers
    - padded dash
    - speed limits
    - police/law
  - POLLUTION
    - unleaded fuel
    - mufflers
    - mass transit
    - safety inspections
  - TRAFFIC
    - freeways
    - passing lanes
    - car pools
    - signs
    - flexible lanes
- BOATS
- BUSES
- BICYCLES
- FEET

Can you think of anything not yet invented that might help solve the problems of safety, pollution, and traffic? Make a list.

ACTIVITY

More Trees

IN A GROUP

Join a small group of classmates to develop trees for one or two of these potential areas of invention. Use the subdivisions given; add your own. Under each subdivision, list problems associated with that area. Under each problem, list solutions or inventions already being tried to help solve that problem.

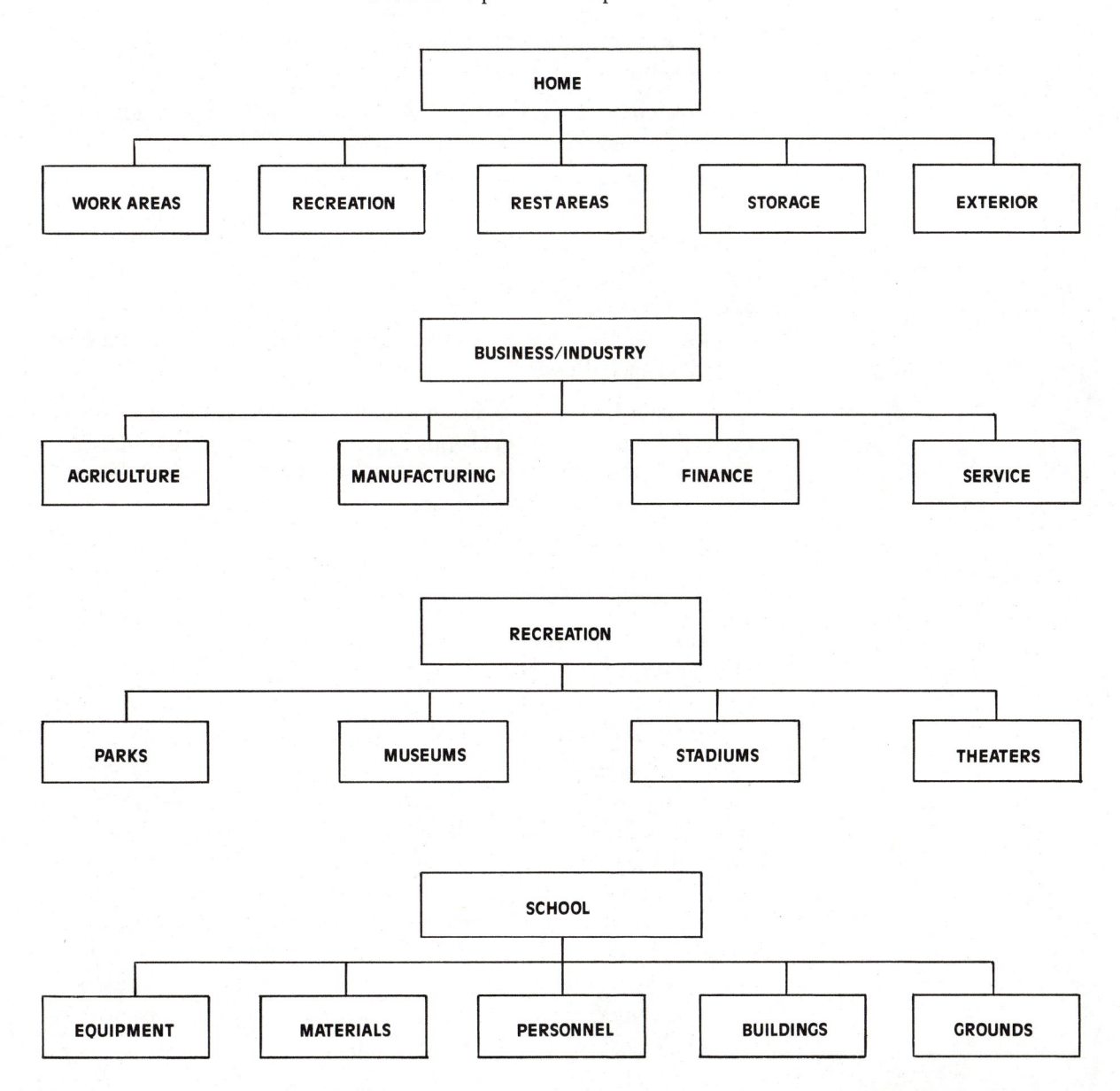

```
                          HOME
    ┌──────────┬──────────┬──────────┬──────────┐
WORK AREAS  RECREATION  REST AREAS  STORAGE  EXTERIOR
```

```
                   BUSINESS/INDUSTRY
       ┌──────────┬──────────┬──────────┐
  AGRICULTURE  MANUFACTURING  FINANCE  SERVICE
```

```
                       RECREATION
       ┌──────────┬──────────┬──────────┐
     PARKS     MUSEUMS    STADIUMS    THEATERS
```

```
                         SCHOOL
    ┌──────────┬──────────┬──────────┬──────────┐
 EQUIPMENT  MATERIALS  PERSONNEL  BUILDINGS  GROUNDS
```

Exploring Possibilities

ACTIVITY
Using Your Trees

ON YOUR OWN

You've practiced grouping your ideas in logical patterns. Now study the trees you and your group made. What inventions come to mind as you think about these unsolved problems? Which tree do you know the most about? Which tree interests you most? Circle interesting problems on your trees.

In your inventor's notebook, write some notes to yourself summarizing problems that are ripe for new inventions. Before you write in your notebook, look at what Charlene wrote in hers:

Transportation: some kind of device to avoid wrecks—radar? vehicles which don't need roads—helicopter? blimp?

Home: security—computer-controlled doors? energy—heat with trash or garbage?

Business: no-cash banks—electronic money? banking at home? shopping centers—any new ideas?

Recreation: ???

Schools: new kind of desk—electric, no paper or pencils, a little keyboard on each desk??

Notice that Charlene has some good ideas, but mostly she has questions. That's good. Her questions can lead her to do more thinking. Now try writing your own notes to yourself. Jot down anything that comes to mind under those headings.

ACTIVITY
Outside Consultants

ON YOUR OWN

Sometimes it is worthwhile to try out new ideas on someone who can be objective—someone who has not been involved in constructing a project, as you have. Businesses often hire consultants to evaluate their procedures. Take your list home with you and see if you can find one or more consultants—adults to share it with, perhaps a parent or an older brother or sister. Ask your consultants what conveniences or devices they wish they had to make their lives easier or safer or more productive. Ask them what problems they have at home, on their way to work, or at work. Try out some of your ideas on them. Put any new ideas you get from consultants in your inventor's notebook.

ON YOUR OWN

By now, you should be about ready to decide on one problem and some ideas for solving it. Reread the section in your inventor's notebook in which you identified problems that were ripe for inventions and about which you made notes for possible solutions. Decide which problem you want to concentrate on. Your problem might or might not be the one that is solvable through the technology you studied most closely.

Write a problem statement that will help you think through what you really hope to do. Before you begin, read Dianne's rough draft of a problem statement:

Problem

More and more homes are being broken into by burglars while people are gone. Burglars break locks or break down doors and enter homes. We need some way to protect the doors to our homes so that they are harder to break into and discourage burglars.

Ideas for a Solution

I want to design a computer-controlled door made of steel that opens only when the owner wants it to. Instead of a key lock, there could be an electronic plate near the door which reads the owner's handprint. The owner puts his hand on the plate, and the computer checks to see if that is the correct hand and then opens the door.

The computer could also keep a record of who comes in and when the door is opened. The computer could also lock the door automatically at night so that no one could enter after a certain time.

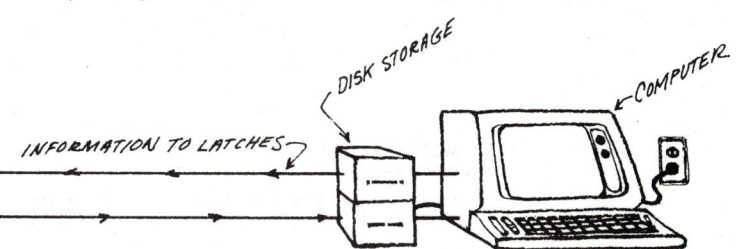

AS A CLASS

Practice your consultant skills on Dianne's ideas. Use the following questions to guide you in judging the clarity of her ideas about the invention:

1. Is Dianne's problem statement clear? Should she add anything to explain it more fully?
2. Is the solution workable? What problems do you think she might have to solve to make it work?
3. Do you have a better idea for solving her problem? What suggestions could you offer?

ACTIVITY

Writing a Problem Statement

ON YOUR OWN

Now try writing your own problem statement as Dianne has done. Begin with a quick draft of the problem. Describe it as fully as you can. Then explain your ideas for a solution. Use sketches and drawings. Include details that will help you think through how the invention will work.

IN A GROUP

Share your problem statement with other members of your technology group. Read it aloud to see if it makes good sense. Show them your sketches. Ask them to act as consultants and give you suggestions. Have them ask you the three questions we asked about Dianne's problem statement.

Inventors' Fair

This next group of activities will help you move from ideas to a product—an invention which is practical and useful. The unit will end with an inventors' fair, a celebration of your good thinking and hard work.

ACTIVITY

Designing Your Own Invention

ON YOUR OWN

You are now the inventor at work. This is your time to work deliberately and creatively to solve a problem you know something about. Don't rush this task or leave it until the night before the fair. Work at home, either alone or with a classmate or an adult who is willing to help. Find the way you work best. The following steps should help you get organized:

1. List alternative solutions.

Look back in your inventor's notebook at your problem statement. Are you satisfied that you have a clear idea of your problem? If not, try rewording. When you are satisfied that the statement is as precise as possible, start listing as many alternative solutions as you can think of. Don't be too concerned about whether the solutions are completely practical. Just list as many as you can.

2. List obstacles.

Once you are satisfied with your list of alternative solutions, make a list of possible difficulties associated with each solution. Why wouldn't the solution work? What complications does it present? Why might people be critical of it? Are your solutions practical? Are they reasonable? List any obstacles beside each solution.

3. Troubleshoot.

Don't throw out any possible solutions yet. Think back over each solution and the obstacles you have listed. How could you overcome the obstacles? Could you invent something else? Could you do it in a different way?

Ask someone to help you if you get stuck—a student, your teacher, another adult. Get another viewpoint. Don't give up on a good idea. Keep tinkering with your invention. Remember Thomas Edison and those thirteen years he put in on the phonograph.

4. Design your invention.

Make a sketch of your invention. Label all of the important parts. Draw it to scale if you can. Use graph paper and let each square equal one foot or one inch. Be sure to indicate on your drawing what your scale is. Be as precise as you can. Take your time. Use a pencil first. Then do an ink drawing.

ACTIVITY

Explaining Your Invention

ON YOUR OWN

Now that you have a satisfactory drawing, it's time to explain in words how your invention works. Using your inventor's notebook, write a draft of your explanation in three parts.

1. Label the first section "The Problem." Review your earlier draft of the problem statement. Revise and refine that statement so that it is a clear and complete statement of the problem. Remember, it must be clear to someone who knows very little about your invention.

2. Label the second section "The Design." In this section explain exactly what your invention is. Explain its important parts and any special features. Refer to your drawing if you need to. Explain exactly how and why it works and how it is a unique solution to the problem.

Exploring Possibilities

3. Label the third section "Possible Problems." Your invention may not be perfect. You may not be able to solve all problems. Even the best inventions have bugs in them. Computers go down, cars won't start on cold mornings, and power failures interrupt service. List problems that could affect your invention. Don't list everything that could go wrong, just the major problems.

ACTIVITY

Revising Your Explanation

IN A GROUP

When you have a draft of your explanation, try it out on some consultants. Ask them to help you remove unnecessary words and add words that make the explanation clearer. Ask them to answer these questions:

1. Is the problem clear? Should I add anything?
2. Is the design section a complete explanation? Have I forgotten any important parts of my invention? Are you confused by any of my terms or drawings?
3. Have I anticipated all major problems? Should I add or remove any possible problems?
4. Do you have any questions about my invention?

ON YOUR OWN

Write a final draft of your explanation. Work to produce a final draft that sounds good and looks good.

Preparing for the Fair

The inventors' fair is a time to display both your invention and your thinking. You need to work on two different products—your individual invention and an explanation of how your mind worked in developing your invention—for the fair. You have already done most of the hard work, thinking. Now it's time to show off your efforts.

ACTIVITY

Displaying Your Individual Invention

ON YOUR OWN

In order for others to understand and appreciate your invention, you need to prepare some kind of picture or model of it. At the fair, inventors' creations should be displayed so that people can walk around and admire them. This means that you need to have something for people to look at besides words. Here are some options you might consider:

1. Graphic displays. You might illustrate your invention with blueprints, drawings, pictures cut from magazines, or photographs.
2. Three-dimensional models. You might make a model from paper, clay, plastic, Styrofoam, wood, cardboard, or any disposable material.
3. Advertisement. A sales brochure or a newspaper or magazine advertisement can show the benefits of your invention.

ACTIVITY

Displaying Your Thinking Processes

ON YOUR OWN

One final job and you are ready for the fair. Because this is a book about thinking and because other people can profit by seeing how your mind worked on the invention, you should share this process with others. How could you show other people how your inventor's mind worked during this project? One idea is to make a kind of map of how you worked on your invention showing when you first got the idea, the things you tried along the way, and how you arrived at the final solution. You did some mapping in Unit I. Remember that birthday map?

If a map or visual display of your thinking doesn't seem to work, you can use your inventor's notebook to make a diary that shows the different stages of your thinking. Look back over your inventor's notebook and make a time line that shows when ideas came to you and how they changed as you developed your invention.

The important point here is to share how you actually thought through the invention problem. Putting that process down on paper is not just for other people. It's also for you. It's a way of learning more about how your own mind works.

Exploring Possibilities

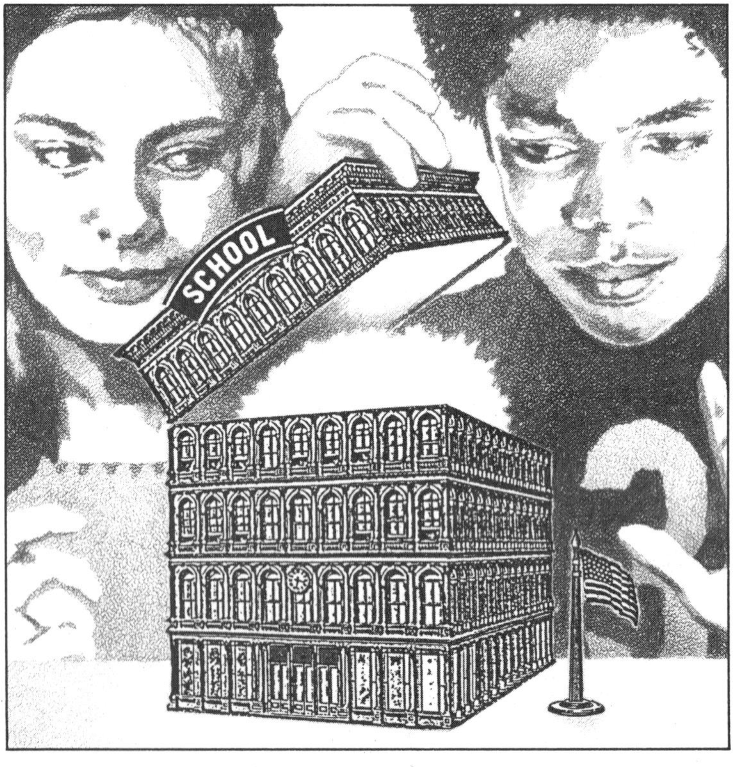
SCHOOL

UNIT III Investigating the Issues

THIS book began with an invitation to start a mental exercise program. If you accepted that invitation, you've already had quite a workout. In the first two units, you've practiced thinking like an artist and like an inventor. You've sharpened your five senses so that they "see" more. You've used your hands to try out creative ideas in your head. In the process you've learned more about how your own mind works. That doesn't mean that you'll discard the skills you practiced in Units I and II. But you're ready to take up a new challenge. That challenge is to think like a researcher.

Different Kinds of Researchers

How do you picture a researcher? Do you see someone wearing a white coat, looking through a microscope in a laboratory? Some researchers do just that. Others spend long hours in a library poring over books and other documents. However, many researchers work beyond the walls of a laboratory or a library. Detectives who solve mysterious cases are researchers. So are reporters who track down the facts for a news story. There are even researchers who investigate what people buy at supermarkets and why.

ACTIVITY

Thinking about Researchers

What do a detective, a newspaper reporter, and someone who studies consumer buying habits have in common? What other kinds of researchers can you think of? How do they work? What guesses can you make about how these researchers think?

ON YOUR OWN

Using these questions to help you get started, write for five minutes about researchers and how they think. Get your ideas down fast and don't worry about form. The point is not to produce a polished piece. It's to capture your own ideas about what researchers do and to make some guesses about how they think. Keep in mind a reporter, a detective, and an analyst of consumers' buying habits.

AS A GROUP

Share your paper with three or four classmates. As papers are read aloud, have a recorder list ideas about how researchers think.

Save your list and add to it as you work through the unit by doing some research of your own.

Investigating the Issues

Tools of the Trade

For the kind of research you'll be doing, you won't need a white coat. You won't even spend much time in the library. However, you will take up the most vital tool of a researcher. This tool isn't as obvious as the artist's paintbrush or the inventor's drawing instruments. In fact, a researcher's primary "tool" is really an attitude—curiosity. Researchers are by definition curious. To the mystery of cancer, they ask "Why?" To the possibility of solar energy, they ask "Why not?" Questions haunt them late at night, plague them when they're eating dinner, and push them to work at odd hours. Researchers just have to KNOW.

Trivial Pursuits

In this unit, you won't be doing complex, scientific research on questions like what causes cancer or how to harness solar energy. Your investigation will be much closer to home. You'll be searching out information right in your own school.

At first, you won't even worry about whether that information is important. In fact, you're going to start with trivia—tidbits that are fun to know but really don't matter much.

As a trivia buff, you'll have lots of company. On many radio talk shows, the host sooner or later tries to stump listeners with a trivia question. Bookstores do a brisk business in paperbacks like *Super Trivia Encyclopedia*. In these books you can find answers to questions like these: Who invented the potato chip? What is Muhammad Ali's CB handle? Who won the Olympic marathon running barefoot? The answers to such questions don't matter much. They just scratch our itch to know.

ACTIVITY

Tracking Down Trivia

What would you like to know about your school? Think small. How many eggs go into that egg salad served in the cafeteria? Who wrote the school fight song? Which teacher has been at the school longest? What book is checked out of the library most often?

WITH A PARTNER

Working with a classmate, make a list of trivia questions about your school. Let your curiosity guide you. List more questions than you can possibly investigate. Now go back and mark the questions that seem most fascinating. How can you find answers to those questions? Who might provide information? Narrow down your list to five questions. Choose two alternates.

Outside class, track down the answer to each of the five questions. Substitute an alternate for any question that can't be answered.

Still working with your partner, write a trivia quiz for your classmates. On the front of a large index card or a half sheet of paper, list your five questions. On the back, write the answers. Your teacher may want you and your partner to try out one or two of your best questions on the class. Ask your teacher about a way to display all the trivia quizzes, perhaps by propping them up along the chalk tray. When time permits, try taking all the other trivia quizzes. How many questions can you answer without looking at the answer key? What are the most interesting pieces of trivia you learned about your school?

Going Beyond

If you enjoyed the trivia hunt, work with several of your friends on one of these optional projects:

- Get permission to start a school trivia bulletin board in the hallway, cafeteria, or library. Invite students from other classes to contribute.
- Make another short trivia quiz. This time, turn the tables: give the answers and see whether your classmates can guess the questions.
- Choose at least five school trivia items you consider newsworthy. Ask the editor of your school paper or the person who makes announcements over the school intercom to feature them in a trivia-of-the-day spot for one week.

Research Workshop

If the trivia hunt aroused your curiosity, you've begun to think like a researcher. You've asked questions and gone out looking for answers. That's a good start, but it's only a start.

Researchers are methodical as well as curious. They work hard at collecting information systematically. They take this information apart and try different ways of putting it back together. They ask "So what?" They weigh the facts and make judgments. Though careful not to jump to conclusions, researchers look for meaning in their findings.

During this unit, you'll work through this whole thinking process. That's a tall order. Don't worry. All you need is practice. That's what this research workshop is all about. Even though you'll be practicing, be sure to save all your work for the researcher's file you'll start later.

There's no better place for a research workshop than your own classroom. There's no better subject than you and your classmates. Together, you make up a small community with interesting characteristics and rich backgrounds and interests. By systematically searching out and pooling personal information, you can create a group profile of your class. Learning more about yourselves as a group will give you a head start in learning more about your school. That's what your big investigation in this unit will be about.

ACTIVITY

Developing a Survey

What you learn from any research depends on the questions you ask. Questions are among the researcher's best tools. They are right up there with an inquiring attitude. Thinking of good questions may be a little hard at first. After all, you probably haven't had much experience asking questions in school. You've been too busy answering them.

Consider the kinds of information you'd really like to collect about your classmates. Your next task will be developing a survey to help you collect it. This survey will not only help you learn more about your classmates; it will also help you learn to ask good questions.

Here's a list of possible topics to help you get started:

- Physical Characteristics
  - Age
  - Sex
  - Eye color
  - Hair color
  - Left-handed or right-handed
- Family
  - Number of brothers
  - Number of sisters
  - Other relatives living with you
  - Pets
- School Experience
  - Years attending this school
  - Previous schools
  - Hardest and easiest subjects
  - Favorite subject
- Likes and Dislikes
  - Music
  - TV shows and movies
  - Food
  - Sports
  - Books

Notice that the topics are grouped into categories. Organizing your questions now will make it easier to compile responses later. You don't want information on brothers, sisters, and pets all jumbled in with likes and dislikes.

IN A GROUP

Work with several classmates to write some questions based on these topics. Writing down your questions will help you make them precise. That's important. If your questions aren't precise, people may not give you the information you really want.

Consider something as simple and straightforward as family. If you ask, "How many people are in your family?" you'll get a number—nothing more. Think what you really want to know. In probing for information about family, you might consider asking questions like these:

What's your position in the family—oldest, youngest, middle, or only child?

How many brothers do you have? How many sisters?

Work together to write your own questions on physical characteristics, family, school experiences, and likes and dislikes, or other categories that you included. Limit yourselves to five questions per category. Do not include questions that might embarrass someone. Have a recorder list those questions and number them. Check out the questions by answering them yourselves. Reword any that aren't clear. Keep working until you are confident that all questions will get the information you want. Then have the recorder read your revised questions aloud so that each group member can make an individual copy. Check to be sure that individual copies are numbered consistently.

Investigating the Issues

ACTIVITY

Survey Exchange

What you just developed is a simple survey. You hear the results of surveys all the time. Surveys tell us the top ten songs and which pain reliever is preferred by four out of five headache sufferers. A survey is simply a set of questions used to collect the same kind of information from a number of people. It's important that this information be collected in a consistent and orderly way. That's why you numbered the questions in each category. Since each member of your group made a copy of your survey, you should have enough for each member of another group.

AS A GROUP

Exchange surveys with another group designated by your teacher. Members of that group will answer your questions, and you will answer theirs.

ON YOUR OWN

To keep things simple, number a clean sheet of paper to correspond with the survey questions you are answering. Working independently, read each question carefully and write your response by the appropriate number. Then return all copies of the survey and all of your responses to the other group. Retrieve your own copy.

ACTIVITY

Compilation

Now you can sift through the results of your probe. The first thing you'll want to do is count the response sheets. Researchers always keep track of how many people respond to their surveys.

If you have only five response sheets, those responses represent only a small sample of all students in your class. They represent an even smaller sample of all students on your grade level. You must be cautious in drawing conclusions about a whole group from such a tiny sample. The larger the sample, the more confident you can be in drawing conclusions.

IN A GROUP

Work with other members of your group to tally the information you've collected. A good plan might be for each person to take one response sheet. A recorder can then call out the number of each question and write responses on a single sheet as they are read aloud.

When you finish, review the tally. Display your findings on oversize paper, one category per sheet. Be sure to start each page with the size of your sample. Otherwise, numbers won't mean much.

For some questions, all you'll need to do is count and report the numbers. In others, it's better to show your findings as averages or percentages. You may even find that some of your information can't be added or averaged because every response is different. If, for example, all seven of the students surveyed gave a different favorite food or movie, there's nothing to tally. That's all right. Just make a list. The important thing is to show as clearly as possible how responses add up.

Physical Characteristics Size of Sample: 7
Average age – 12.1 years
Sex – 57% girls 43% boys
Hair color – 2 brown 2 black 2 blond 1 red

AS A CLASS

Display your charts for the rest of the class. Nearby, post a copy of your survey questions. Study charts prepared by other groups. What kinds of information appear on more than one chart? Compare similar information. Also compare the questions used to gather the information. Did some questions seem to work better than others? If so, why? As you study the charts and think through these questions, jot down notes.

ACTIVITY

More Compilation

Now, it's time to do another compiling job—a master chart of the class responses. This job will be harder because you'll be merging more information. But the results should be worth the efforts. They will represent your total class response and a larger sample of your grade level. They'll give you a sharper picture of your own group.

AS A CLASS

Help your teacher make a chalkboard compilation of the information displayed on all the charts. In the process, you'll *really* be thinking like a researcher. You'll be getting more advanced practice in putting small pieces of information together and seeing how they add up. That's an important thinking skill.

Investigating the Issues

ACTIVITY
Interpreting Results

> AS A CLASS

Take a few minutes to discuss the information compiled on the chalkboard. Remember that the purpose of your practice survey is to learn as much as possible about your class as a small community within the school. What information about your little community seems most interesting? Does anything surprise you? Do you think the information collected at another school would be similar? Think of yourself. In what ways do you see yourself as a typical member of the group? In what ways do you think you are different?

Researchers don't usually keep their findings to themselves. If they've asked good questions, collected lots of information, and compiled that information carefully, their work is worth sharing. So is yours.

Going Beyond

Choose one of these ways to share your class profile:

- Write a feature story for your school or neighborhood newspaper. Think of that story as a class photograph using words instead of film. If you prefer, do an individual verbal snapshot: "If you know Ronnie, you have a good picture of all eighth-graders..."
- Draw a cartoon of the "typical" or "average" boy or girl suggested by your findings. Add labels or captions to give vital statistics—for example, "one of 2-1/2 children in family; likes pepperoni pizza."
- Write a letter to students in your grade at another school. Report what you have learned about your own class. Ask them to reply, commenting on how they think their class is like yours and how it is different.

School Project

Now that you've finished your workshop and learned how to organize a search for answers, you're ready for a major research project. The rest of the activities in this unit will guide you and your classmates through a comprehensive study of your school. The project will result in a State of the School Report—a written document that might inform your class, school administrators, and others about the strengths of your school and recommend some ways to make it even better.

Think about your school for a minute. How fully could you describe it to someone who was new in town? What do you already know, and what would you need to find out?

How many students are enrolled in your school? How many boys? How many girls? How many on each grade level?

How many teachers does your school have? On the average, how long have they taught? What do they like best about the school? What do they think could be improved?

How many administrators work in your school? How many support staff like counselors, librarians, and nurses? Who else helps keep the school running smoothly? What does your principal see as important goals for your school?

How does the community view the school? Are community members proud of it? Are there things they'd like to see changed? Did any of them go to school there? How has the school changed?

What shape is your building in? Have there been any new wings or additions? What sports facilities exist?

The answers to these and other questions will form the basis of your State of the School Report, which you will present to your principal and others. The report will be a careful and honest picture of your school emphasizing its strengths and recommending ways to make it even better.

Such a comprehensive report is too big a job for one or two people. Your entire class will work together as a research team to do the legwork and write the report. This project will require everyone's best thinking.

ACTIVITY

Making a Researcher's File

Before you become a part of a research team, take some time to gather the tools and supplies you'll need to work efficiently. One of the most important, and for some people, the most difficult steps in research is getting organized. If you are a person who tends to lose books and misplace notes, getting organized is especially important to you.

ON YOUR OWN

Your first task is to find or make something to hold supplies and later your research notes. An unused briefcase or attaché case hiding in an attic or closet at home might be perfect. Maybe someone at your house has an old knitting bag, beach bag, or small backpack. Accordion folders, the kind that expand as you fill them and have a string tie to keep the contents secure, might work. You can improvise by finding just the right shaped box or container.

Take a serious tour through your home to see what is available. Remember that your file should be sturdy enough to hold all of your materials and notes. It must also be portable so that you can carry it with you as you do the fieldwork for your research.

Put your name on your file and give it a professional look. Stock it with a note pad, a package of note cards (any size), four or five pencils, several pens, and felt-tip highlighters in several colors. As your research moves ahead and your file begins to fill up, you may want to add dividers to organize your papers. Start your file with all the work you did during the research workshop.

ACTIVITY

Keeping an Investigator's Log

ON YOUR OWN

One more thing: find a small tablet to serve as an investigator's log. Each day, enter the date and jot down the specific tasks you are working on. Add notes about problems that crop up or techniques that you learn. Think of your log as a research diary. Your daily entries should provide a record of your work on the State of the School Report.

Fact-Finding Teams

The research business is just about to become more complicated, so stay alert and pay attention to the following organizational plan. You will be assigned to one of five teams:

1. Students
2. School Administration
3. Faculty
4. Immediate Community
5. General Public

These five different teams will become a data base or a source of information for your fact-finding teams to survey. If you have been assigned to the Student, School Administration, or Faculty team, you will conduct your survey in the school, passing out and collecting survey forms in some efficient way that doesn't disrupt regular work.

If you have been assigned to the Immediate Community team, you can work in pairs or larger groups to survey people who live in the neighborhood around your school, perhaps in a four- or five-block area. You might hand out survey forms door-to-door or leave them by mailboxes.

If you are in the General Public team, you can work in pairs or groups to decide on a location where community people come and go. Consider a shopping center, a supermarket, a discount store, a theater complex, a town square, or a courthouse—any place that permits surveys to be taken. Your people will fill out their survey forms on the spot.

Categories of Questions

During the research workshop, you practiced grouping your questions by category. When you organized your questions, it was much easier to classify your classmates' responses. During this project, you will collect much more information. That's why careful organization is even more important now. Try developing your questions from the following four categories:

1. Buildings and Grounds
Questions in this category relate to appearance, size, and facilities.

2. Instructional Program
Questions in this category will focus on the kinds of courses offered in the school.
3. Support Services
Questions in this category center on all the people who help make the school more efficient, pleasant, and productive.
4. Student Activities
Questions in this category concentrate on opportunities for students to pursue special interests.

Accentuating the Positive

Probably everyone has complained about a school at one time or another. Recently schools have been criticized by newspapers, national reports, and political leaders. Since most educators are working very hard and stretching limited financial resources to accomplish a great deal, they are understandably sensitive about such criticism. That's one of the many reasons your group must be careful to approach this study in a positive way. Your purpose is to help everyone understand your school better, not to criticize teachers or attack administrators. Actually, a good survey can *help* your school by making it more visible and making people feel involved. To ensure that this study is constructive and well received, your questions should be of two basic types:

1. What are the strengths of our school? What do we do well? What successes have we had?

2. How can we make our school better? What suggestions could we offer to help teachers? administrators? students?

Formats for Questions

As you already know, a survey is a series of questions designed to collect information. In developing questions for your classroom survey earlier in the unit, you probably used different kinds of questions. Some were simple yes/no questions. Do you have any brothers? Do you have any sisters? Some questions asked the person to fill in a number or short answer. How many brothers do you have? ____ How many sisters? ____ Some questions were stated so that the person could simply check an answer. How many brothers do you have? ____ 0 ____ 1 ____ 2 ____ 3 ____ 4 ____ 5 or more. Some questions may have asked the person to rank items. In order, list your top five favorite musical groups. In order, list your three favorite fast foods.

One other kind of question you might consider is called a Likert-type question. A Likert-type question is really a statement which respondents read and then check how they feel about it. For example:

Lanier Middle School has an attractive, well-kept campus.

No Opinion	Strongly Disagree	Disagree	Agree	Strongly Agree
0	1	2	3	4

The Likert-type question has two advantages. It is easy to tally, and it tells the researcher how strongly a respondent feels about the answer.

You now have five different formats of questions to consider for your survey:

1. Yes/no
2. Short answer
3. Check the answer
4. Ranked answers
5. Likert-type answer

The kinds of questions you develop and the formats you choose will depend upon the type of information you are gathering.

Focus on Respondents

Asking the right question is important. So is asking the right people. It is your job as a researcher to match the right questions with the right people. Students, faculty, administrators, and community members can all provide valuable information for your State of the School Report. But they will provide different information because they each know different things and see your school from different points of view.

Investigating the Issues 75

Let's say you're going to ask questions about the instructional program in your school. How will you word those questions for the group you are surveying? Here are some examples to help you get started.

Students

1. Are you satisfied with the kinds of courses you are taking this year?

    (Check one) _____ YES _____ NO _____ NOT SURE

2. What is the most enjoyable class you are taking this year?

    (Check one) _____ Math _____ Science _____ English _____ Social Studies
    _____ Art _____ Music _____ P.E. _____ OTHER (Please list.)

3. I feel I am getting a good education at this school.

(Circle one)	(DON'T KNOW) NO OPINION	STRONGLY DISAGREE	DISAGREE	AGREE	STRONGLY AGREE
	0	1	2	3	4

Faculty

1. Do you have adequate books and materials to teach your courses?

    (Check one) _____ YES _____ NO _____ NOT SURE

2. What resources would help you do your job better?

    (Check one or more) _____ more books _____ more supplies _____ better facilities _____ I have no real needs.

3. Do you think homework is important?

    (Check one) _____ Yes, very important _____ Yes, some homework is good. _____ Sometimes, I give little homework. _____ No, I never give homework.

4. I think students get a good education at this school.

(Circle one)	(DON'T KNOW) NO OPINION	STRONGLY DISAGREE	DISAGREE	AGREE	STRONGLY AGREE
	0	1	2	3	4

    Comments: _____

School Administration

1. List your top three priorities for our school. _____
   _____
   _____

2. The program I am most proud of in our school is _____ .

3. If you had the money, what is the next thing you would do to improve our school program?
   _____

Immediate Community

1. How do you feel about homework?

   (Check one) ____ Students need more of it.   ____ Students have too much of it.   ____ It seems about right.   ____ I don't know.

2. What do you think are the most important courses in _____ School?

   (Rank these 1–9)
   ____ Math   ____ English   ____ P.E.
   ____ Science   ____ Foreign language ____ Music and art
   ____ Social studies ____ Drama   ____ Career courses

General Public

1. If you were going to give _____ School a grade for its efforts to educate young people, what would it be?

   (Check one)   ____ A   ____ B   ____ C   ____ D   ____ F

2. What good things have you heard about _____ School?

   (Please list) _____
   _____
   _____

3. Would you support higher taxes to lower class size at _____ School?

   (Check one)   ____ YES   ____ NO   ____ NOT SURE

As you can see from these sample questions, the options are endless. You can ask the same question in different ways for different groups.

Investigating the Issues

ACTIVITY

Developing the Survey

Now that you've explored some formats for asking questions and considered ways of fitting those questions to a particular group, you are ready to roll up your sleeves and develop a survey form. Fortunately, you won't be tackling the job alone. You'll work with one of the five fact-finding teams already organized by your teacher.

> **IN A GROUP**

Your first job as a research team is to brainstorm a long list of questions that will help identify strengths of your school and ways it might be improved. Here, you have a choice. One is to brainstorm according to the categories suggested earlier—building and grounds, instructional program, support services, and student activities. The other is to let the brainstorming be more freewheeling. If you take the second option, you can then examine your list and code questions according to the same four categories.

In either case, choose your best questions. Your survey should probably have no more than five questions per category. That adds up to a total of twenty questions for your survey forms.

Here is a step-by-step plan for drawing up your survey form:

1. Generate questions.
2. Group under four categories.
3. Narrow to five per category.
4. Rewrite questions choosing from various formats. Remember to accentuate the positive.
5. Read your questions aloud. Answer them yourselves.
6. Complete checklist for survey.
7. Type up survey. Proofread for spelling and form. Duplicate.

The next-to-last step on that plan requires a bit of explanation. The following checklist is a last-minute inspection of your work—in this case, your survey form. It gives you a chance to step back and evaluate what you've done. More importantly, it gives you a chance to correct any weaknesses. This kind of checking is part of thinking like a researcher.

Here is a suggested checklist for your survey:

The Survey Checklist

	1	2	3	4	5

CONTENT

| Questions don't get to the heart of the matter. They miss the target. | | Questions are nearly on target. Some need stronger focus on what really matters. | | Questions are right on target. Answers will tell us exactly what we need to know about this school. |

FORMAT

| Still rough. Questions could confuse people. Results could be a mess to compile! | | So far so good. Sharpening wording and reorganizing the format could make compiling results a lot easier. | | Good job. The format is sharp and well chosen. Compilation of results should be easy. |

APPROPRIATENESS

| The survey team could have big problems with these questions. | | Most questions are appropriate to the knowledge and viewpoint of the group being surveyed. | | Survey fits the group. It asks about what they know and feel about the school. |

Notice the numbers across the top. These numbers represent ratings. A *1* indicates major problems. In effect, it tells you to go back to the drawing board. A *5* indicates top quality. It tells you that your survey is polished and ready to go. Anything between indicates the need for some fine-tuning here and there.

Use the numbers on the checklist to rate your team's survey on content, format, and appropriateness. Share these ratings with your teacher and see how they compare to his or hers. Make any necessary adjustments. Then make sure that the survey begins with a clear set of written instructions. If surveys are not to be completed and returned on the spot, include a return name and address.

Investigating the Issues 79

ACTIVITY
Conducting the Survey

IN A GROUP

Before setting out for the school cafeteria, faculty lounge, principal's office, or a nearby shopping mall to conduct your survey, take another few minutes to coordinate plans. As a group, decide on a minimum and maximum number of people to be surveyed by each person. Especially in the case of teachers and administrators, be sure that the same people won't be approached by more than one team member. Agree on some ground rules to avoid interrupting people's regular activities or taking too much of their time. Be sure you can meet the deadline set by your teacher for completion and return of all survey forms.

ON YOUR OWN

As you collect information, be sure to explain your purpose to people you survey. Offer to share results. If surveys are being completed on the spot, check to be sure all questions have been answered. Thank each person for taking time to participate in the survey. Place each completed form in your researcher's file for safekeeping.

ACTIVITY
Adding Up Results

AS A GROUP

When the survey has been completed, meet with your team to compile results. Count the completed forms to determine the size of your sample. Tally answers on a blank survey form.

Take a few minutes to examine the information you have compiled. Have a recorder write down your answers to these questions: On what survey items do you find the most agreement among respondents? The most disagreement? What questions received the most positive responses? The most negative? Are there any responses so scattered that they almost cancel each other out? What pattern of responses seems most significant? Most surprising?

In dealing with these questions, you've moved from merely tallying information into interpreting it. In other words, you've begun to consider what all that information means. You're trying to make sense of it. That's an important kind of thinking—especially for a researcher.

Plan a brief presentation to share your findings with the rest of the class. Begin by identifying the group your team surveyed and giving the size of your sample. Then share highlights from your compiled responses. Include tentative conclusions about strengths of the school as identified by the group surveyed. Also include possible needs for improvement. Be prepared to turn in your tally of survey results.

ACTIVITY

Merging Viewpoints

In listening to reports of other teams, did you notice any contrasts in how different groups view your school? For example, did students and teachers have opposite points of view about homework or extracurricular activities? Were community members who live near the school more concerned with the appearance of the buildings and grounds than were members of the general public? Your State of the School Report should fairly represent all points of view.

Your next major job is to merge results of all five surveys. For this task, you will be organized into new teams, one for each category of information you collected: Buildings and Grounds, Instructional Program, Support Services, and Student Activities. Each new team should include at least one person from each of the old fact-finding teams. That way, all new teams will have someone to answer questions about each set of data.

Your teacher will either cut the five tally sheets apart by category or make copies of all tally sheets for each team. In either case, you will be provided with compiled information collected in your category on all surveys. Your job is to put all of that information together.

Since the content and format of each survey was different, that job won't be easy. It will require careful interpretation and your best judgment. A systematic approach will help.

| IN A GROUP |

Begin with a careful reading of all survey results. Notice questions that seem to be getting at the same point. For example, if your team is responsible for merging information on the instructional program, you might notice this item on the student survey: "What is the most enjoyable class you are taking this year?" On the survey of the immediate community, you notice this item: "What do you think are the most important courses in school?" Though these questions are different, they both ask about course preferences.

Investigating the Issues

Find such related items in different surveys. Color-coding is one good way to keep track of corresponding items. Just mark items that go together with the same color highlighter. Use a different color for each pair or cluster of questions.

Discuss each pair or cluster of items. Focus on compiled responses. Do responses differ a great deal across groups, or is there some measure of consensus? Taken together, what do all the responses add up to?

Again, let's say that you are compiling information on the instructional program in your school. When asked a Likert-type question about how good an education they were getting, students agreed that they were getting a good education. The average was *3* on a *4*-point scale. On the same kind of questions, faculty strongly agreed; they responded with straight *4*s. When asked to grade the school on its efforts to educate young people, the general public gave the school a B+. What can you generalize from these three sets of responses?

As you work through results of the five surveys, have a recorder keep a list of your tentative conclusions. Beside each conclusion, the recorder can jot down the items on each survey that support it.

Finally, go back over your conclusions. Try to sort them into two groups—strengths and possible needs for improvement. As a team, begin translating those needs into specific recommendations for improving the school. Keep working until you have two lists that can be supported by survey results—one of your school's strengths and one of recommendations for making your school even better. Order your lists according to importance. Be sure all points of view are represented.

Present both lists to the class. Back them up with survey results. Build in any good suggestions offered by classmates.

ACTIVITY

Preparing the Report

Do you feel like a veteran researcher? You should. Take a minute to congratulate yourself. You've almost finished a very ambitious project.

As the title of this unit promised, you've investigated real issues. You've done a here-and-now research project right where you live—in your own school. As a result, you understand your school better. Now you are ready to publish what you have learned so that others will understand it better. You are also ready to make some constructive recommendations.

Throughout this project, you and your classmates have worked as a team. You'll also work as a team to publish the results of your study. Since there's a great deal to be done, it's best to organize committees to work with an editor-in-chief appointed by your teacher. The editor-in-chief will be responsible for writing an introduction explaining the purpose of the report and for coordinating the work of these committees:

- *Writing Teams*—Two or three people from each topic team (Building and Grounds, Instructional Program, Support Services, Student Activities) will be responsible for writing on that topic for the report. Each writing team will also be responsible for writing an introductory explanation of the topic. This will be followed by a list of major strengths identified in the survey and recommendations for improving that particular function of the school. The entire section—introductory overview, strengths, and recommendations—should be given to the editor-in-chief and the teacher for approval.

- *Publication Team*—Volunteers or appointees will type, proofread, and reproduce copies of the entire report. This team should include several good typists or word processors. If not, team members may recruit relatives or friends who are willing to help. This team is also responsible for proofreading the manuscript, reproducing it as directed by the teacher, and collating pages.

- *Cover and Graphics Team*—Volunteers or appointees will design and mass produce covers and provide any graphics or pictures needed to illustrate the report.

Going Beyond

If time allows, you may wish to complete one of these optional activities. Your work will contribute a nice "extra" to the State of the School Report:

- Collaborate with several classmates in making up a brief survey to collect biographical data from all members of the faculty. Include questions about out-of-school interests and activities. After getting permission, place a survey form in each teacher's mailbox. Attach a brief explanatory note and instructions for return. Use survey responses to compile a faculty directory to include

as an appendix, a section added at the end of the report.
- Take photographs to illustrate each section of the report.
- Perhaps working with a partner, research the history of the school. Get leads from the principal, the school librarian, veteran teachers, and older relatives or neighbors who attended the school. Write a school history to include in the introduction to the report.
- Draw a map of the campus and perhaps a floor plan of the building. Contribute it to the Buildings and Grounds section of the report.

ACTIVITY

Setting Priorities

Publishing your State of the School Report will take time. Some of the committee work will have to be done outside of class. Don't get impatient. The product should be worth the effort.

AS A CLASS

As work on publication progresses, take one more look at your findings. List on the chalkboard all recommendations for making your school even better than it is. Include the recommendations from all four sections.

Your final task is to select five recommendations and rank them according to priority. This ranking will represent the bottom line of your research project—the big "So what?" or "Where do we go from here?" These recommendations will be proposed for actions in your school.

Selecting and ranking your recommendations will take some hard thinking. You'll have to weigh one need against another. You'll have to make some value judgments. You'll have to decide what's realistic as well as what's desirable.

A good starting point is to reach an agreement about all the recommendations strictly on the basis of soundness and importance. Where are changes needed most? What recommended actions would have the best payoff in terms of improving the school?

After ranking recommendations according to soundness and importance, consider the issue of practicality. Give each item a +, √, or x according to the criteria below:

+   Thoroughly realistic—May take some time and money, but neither seems unreasonable. No major obstacles to this proposed change.

√   Difficult but possible—May take longer and cost more, but benefits are worth it. Problems can be overcome.

x   Impractical—Price tag too high. Too many obstacles in the way.

If your top five priorities are rated +, you have no reason to change them. You'll want to take a close look at those with a √ and an even closer look at those with an x. Weigh importance against practicality. As you do so, debate among yourselves. Be sure to consider all the issues. Then make a consensus list of your top five recommendations ranked in order of priority. Title your list "A Proposal for Action." Include it in your State of the School Report.

ACTIVITY

Publishing the Report

We've said before that researchers rarely keep good findings to themselves. They want others to share the results of their investigations. They want their efforts to count.

Now it is time to publish. The number of copies you have to share will depend on lots of things. Your teacher has arranged for you to publish as many copies as possible within available resources. Now you will have the pleasure of distributing those copies.

> **AS A CLASS**

Decide who should receive copies of the report. Certainly you'll want to present a copy to your principal. If your principal approves, you may circulate copies to the faculty and others. Also consider placing a copy in the school library and presenting one to the parent-teacher group in your school. However you decide to distribute your report, be sure each copy is accompanied by a cover letter.

Investigating the Issues   85

Going Beyond

Even if you have a limited distribution, results of your study can be widely shared. Work with a partner or a small group on one of these projects to publicize your work.

- Write a feature story or an editorial about your State of the School Report for the school newspaper.
- Script an assembly presentation giving highlights of your report. If assembly time is not available, request time during the morning announcements over the intercom.
- Prepare a panel discussion on your research project and seek permission to present it for the parent-teacher organization in your school or for a local civic group. Be sure to include your "Proposal for Action" and end with a question-answer session.
- Seek permission to report your research project at a regular faculty meeting. If permitted, ask for suggestions on how results might be further publicized in the school.

ACTIVITY

Looking Back

Before putting away your researcher's file and closing out your investigator's log for good, take a few minutes to think through what you've done in this unit. What does it really mean to think like a researcher? How accurate were your preliminary guesses in that five-minute writing you did at the beginning of the unit?

ON YOUR OWN

Review your log and retrace your steps in investigating your own school. As a final entry in your log, make a list of the things you feel you've done best. Make another list of things you haven't done so well. In both cases, be very specific. Try to label the kind of thinking involved—for example, "I had trouble color-coding. I couldn't figure out which questions on all those different surveys got at the same point. I guess it's hard for me to see how different pieces of information fit together."

IN A GROUP

Share your entry with a partner, a small group of friends, or the whole class. Brainstorm some ways to practice skills that still need work. Be prepared to hand in your log so that your teacher can make further suggestions.

A Final View

Now that you've practiced thinking like a researcher, are you wondering what you can do with those skills in everyday life? Take a minute for one more inventory of what you have done. You've sharpened your curiosity. You've practiced asking good questions and organizing a search for answers. You've practiced taking information apart and putting it back together in different ways. You've practiced interpreting data and making judgments. In other words, you've practiced critical thinking.

Aren't those the skills you need in school every day? Don't you need to ask questions when there are gaps in what you know? Don't you need to fit pieces of information together? Interpret? Evaluate? Make judgments? In a way, school is one big research project.

So are decision-making tasks like deciding what camera to buy or where to go on a family vacation. Thinking like a researcher is indeed everyday business.

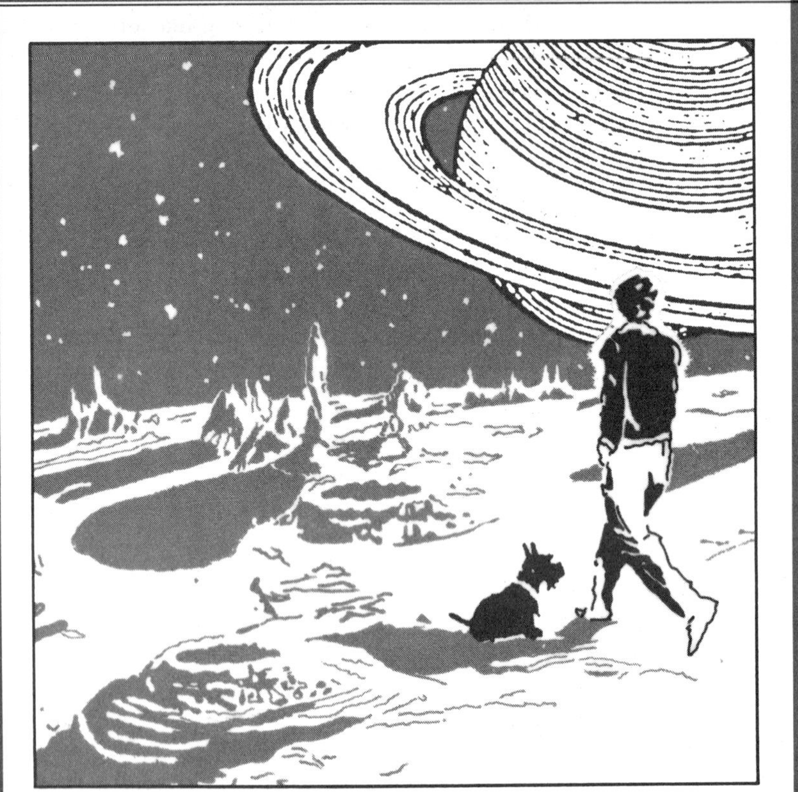

UNIT IV Probing the Future

IMAGINING the future may seem a lot like daydreaming. In a way, it is. Realistically, we can't see ourselves and predict what our lives will be like much beyond the next few years. Think how hard it is to look back. When someone pulls out the old family pictures, we say, "I can't believe I looked like that." It's even harder to look ahead. Don't you find it difficult to imagine what you will be like after high school, much less in ten or twenty years?

But looking ahead is an important kind of thinking. As our world continues to change faster and faster, we have to get better at planning ahead. We must be prepared for the kind of chain reaction set off by revolutions like the invention of the automobile. Back then, no one foresaw the problems of pollution, congestion, and safety. As a result many of our cities face serious environmental problems from the number of automobiles on their streets and freeways.

Not planning ahead has created problems for many of America's factory workers in basic industries like steel, coal, railroads, and auto production. Some of these workers have been replaced by robots or computers. Losing their jobs to technology after a lifetime of commitment causes many to feel a sense of helplessness.

Futurists are people who look beyond the present and help us plan ahead for change. Futurists try to anticipate what might happen, forecast changes, and even think of ways to solve problems before they arise.

In this unit you will begin thinking like a futurist—forecasting changes in your own life, predicting the results of such changes, and considering alternative solutions for possible problems. You will imagine and plan a future you'd really like for yourself and others. As futurists like to say, you will prepare to invent your own future.

Futures File

As a working futurist, you're going to need a place to keep all of your materials and supplies. This file should be large enough to hold lots of clippings from magazines and newspapers. Futurists are always on the lookout for news of trends, like shrinking birth rate, and information about new technological developments, like laser surgery or electronic banking. Futurists are also on the alert for changing uses of the environment, like the harvesting of the Amazon rain forest, which may alter world ecology. You can see why futurists read newspapers and magazines and clip out any articles that give clues to future changes. Your own futures file will be the place to keep similar information you collect.

Your futures file will also be the place to keep your own work. That work will help you get ready for the major project in this unit. That will be the writing of a scenario—your imaginary version of the way you think the world might be at some point in the future. Like a professional futurist, you'll share this story in a futurists' forum. You and your classmates will pool your scenarios. That way you can consider lots of alternative futures. Between now and the forum, think of your futures file as a place to collect alternatives, both your own and those of others.

ACTIVITY

Making Your File

ON YOUR OWN

To help your teacher keep the room uncluttered and to make your filing system work for you, find a standard-sized shoe box with a lid. There may be time in class to personalize your file. Begin by making a file label for the end of the box. Your teacher will tell you what information to put on the label, but it should look something like this:

FUTURES FILE
Jacobs, Sarah 5th period Mr. Burnette

Be sure to print your label in letters large enough to be read from across the room.

The second item of business with your futures file is to decorate the lid of your box. Use drawings if you like or pictures and words clipped from magazines if a collage is more your style. In either case, show what things will be important to your life in 2010. How will you spend your time? What will you value? What worries will you have? How will your life have changed? Create a design for the lid of your futures file which gives others a picture of what you will be like in about twenty-five years.

WITH A PARTNER

Share your design with a partner and explain what various pictures mean. Talk about what you think your life will be like. Compare your personal view of the future with your partner's. How are they alike? How are they different? Is your picture an optimistic or hopeful one? Is it pessimistic? Or is it full of uncertainty?

The Big Picture

So far, you have thought of the future in personal terms. That's good. But how you see yourself in the future depends a great deal on how you see the future itself. During this unit, you'll look at the future from lots of different perspectives. You'll begin by stepping back and looking at it from a distance. You'll be like a photographer looking at a big subject through a wide-angle lens.

It's not easy to think about something as complicated as the future. One way to tackle such a huge idea is to compare it to something simpler and more familiar. That's what you'll do with the future. You'll explore your own view of the future by comparing it to something more familiar. This use of one thing to explain or clarify another is called *metaphor.*

ACTIVITY

Metaphors for the Future

ON YOUR OWN

Here are four metaphors for the future. A metaphor is a description of a thing in terms of something it is like. As your teacher reads them aloud, jot down points of agreement and disagreement with each:

1. The future is a giant roller coaster on a dark night. It has lots of ups and downs, twists and turns. We can often guess what direction we're headed and sometimes see the section of track right in front of us. Looking ahead into the dark doesn't do us much good, though. The future, like the roller coaster track, is fixed. We are locked into our seats, and nothing will change the predetermined course in front of us. All we can do is ride it out.

2. The future is a powerful river. It surges forward, carrying us with it. When we try to change the course of history, our attempts are like pebbles tossed into the water. They cause a brief splash and a few ripples, but make no real difference. The river's course *can* be changed but only by natural disasters like earthquakes or by the massive work of many people and machines working together. About all individuals can do is adapt to the flow of the river. We can look for sandbars and whirlpools to avoid and steer our way through the rapids.

3. The future is a vast ocean. We can sail across it toward many destinations. Where we go and how we get there is up to us. In navigating the future, we can take advantage of strong currents of change. We can adapt to the winds of chance. We can move cautiously through fog or uncharted waters. Good sailors who keep a sharp lookout will arrive safely at their destination—that is, if there's no typhoon or other disaster which can be neither predicted nor avoided.

4. The future is a gigantic dice game. It's entirely random. Every moment of every day, millions of things happen that could have happened another way and led to a different future. A bullet is deflected and kills one person instead of another. A scientist noticing a spoiled culture either throws it away or takes a closer look and discovers penicillin. A spy breaking into an office at the Watergate hotel remembers to remove tape from a door latch, or he forgets it and changes

Probing the Future 93

the course of American history. The future, like a dice game, is pure chance. All we can do is play the game and hope for good luck.

WITH A PARTNER

Discuss these questions: Which of these metaphors best expresses your view of the future? In other words, with which view do you most strongly agree? With which do you most strongly disagree? Why?

IN A GROUP

Your teacher will poll the class to see which metaphor for the future is most and least popular. Form a group with other members of your class who chose the same metaphor. Together, list reasons for your choice and present them to the rest of the class. Make the best case you can for viewing the future as a roller coaster, a river, an ocean, or a dice game.

ACTIVITY
Brainstorming Metaphors

AS A CLASS

Brainstorm a list of other things the future might be like. For example, you might think of the future as a blank sheet of paper or as a superhighway that branches in many directions. Your teacher will appoint a recorder to make a chalkboard list of your own metaphors for the future. Make the list as long as you can. Then go back and talk about each proposed metaphor and the view of the future it suggests.

ON YOUR OWN

Which metaphor seems to you most striking and most appropriate? Explore the comparison by jotting down as many details as possible. If you picture the future as a system of superhighways, your list might begin like this:

- traffic moves fast
- gets more crowded all the time
- have to move with flow of cars
- driver has to watch for signs
- anticipate junctions

When you have a good jot list, develop your ideas into a paragraph like the ones on pages 93–94.

WITH A PARTNER

Try out your metaphor by reading it aloud to a partner. Does the metaphor work? Does the paragraph have enough detail to create a vivid picture of the future? What might make the comparison clearer and more interesting?

ON YOUR OWN

After your partner has made some suggestions, write another draft and save it in your futures file.

Going Beyond

Put your metaphor into a different form for classroom display. Choose one of these options or one of your own:

- Shape your metaphor into a list poem. Take out extra words. Arrange lines in an interesting way.

- Express your metaphor in a series of drawings, with a caption or title. Arrange and title your work.
- Using pictures clipped from magazines and any other materials you wish, compose a collage that expresses your metaphor.

Guessing the Future

Futurists do not pretend to be fortune tellers: they don't try to *predict* the future with crystal balls or star charts. They try to make informed guesses about possible futures. They think about future alternatives rather than about the future.

The next exercise is designed to help you practice one of a futurist's most important activities: forecasting. Forecasts are guesses about what might happen.

ACTIVITY

Forecasting

ON YOUR OWN

To begin this activity, you need to make yourself a large time line. You probably remember time lines from studying history. Take a full sheet of paper and make your time line stretch across its full length. Copy this example.

Now ——— 1990 ——— 2000 ——— 2025 ——— Distant Future

Now study the following list of things which may happen in the future. Think about each item carefully. When do you think it might become a reality? Find that point on your time line. Place key words there to stand for that item. You might want to use a pencil in case you decide to move some items.

1. Schools operate on a year-round schedule with short, staggered vacations for students and teachers.
2. Schools become unnecessary or obsolete as students do most of their learning on computers in their own homes or in shopping malls.
3. Most homes have television sets that project three-dimensional images.
4. Robots take over routine household chores such as cooking and cleaning.
5. Credit cards and electronic banking make money a thing of the past.
6. Newspapers, magazines, and all mail are delivered by home computers to be read from the screen or printed electronically. Postal workers are obsolete.
7. Much of the world's farming and manufacturing takes place on orbiting space stations.

8. Ninety percent of the world's people live in cities.
9. Many large cities have domes for weather control.
10. Energy problems are solved once and for all by new ways of harnessing solar energy.
11. The average life expectancy in America is 150 years.
12. People typically work a twenty-hour week and retire at age thirty-five.
13. Cloning is perfected and becomes widespread.
14. Almost any organ in the human body can be surgically replaced with an artificial one.
15. By law, no family can have more than two children.

IN A GROUP

When you are satisfied with your time line, your teacher will ask you to work in groups to compare your guesses about the future with your classmates' guesses. All group members should discuss some of the guesses they are most confident about and least confident about. As other group members share their guesses, ask them to explain why they think something will happen. Don't argue about guesses. There are no right or wrong answers here.

Going Beyond

- Select a point on your time line and pretend that you operate a museum full of obsolete things from the past. What things will be in your museum? Why have they become obsolete? Make a list of some of the things in your museum and the things that replaced them.

- Select a point on your time line and develop some likely newspaper headlines for that date. What events or discoveries or changes might make the headlines in 2010 or 2050?

ACTIVITY

The Future and You

ON YOUR OWN

Imagine that a time machine has just propelled you into the future. You are twenty-five years old. What year will that be? Take a look at the person you hope to be at age twenty-five. How do you hope to be living? What does your time line suggest might be possible by that time? Think about these questions:

1. Where would you like to be living? In what state or country? In what kind of community? Describe that place and tell why you want to live there.

2. Do you live in a house, a highrise condo, a mobile home, or some other kind of dwelling? How does it look? What worksaving devices does it have?

3. Who else is in your family? Are you single or married? Do you have or plan to have children?

4. What kind of work do you do? Where do you do it? Why did you choose this kind of job?

5. How do you spend your leisure time? How much do you have? What do you enjoy about your special hobbies or favorite kinds of entertainment?

ACTIVITY

Future Autobiography

ON YOUR OWN

Your next task is to write an autobiography. Most autobiographies tell what has already happened to a person. This one will tell what you would like to happen in the future. You'll write this autobiography in two installments—the first describing yourself and your life-style at age twenty-five, the second at age fifty. Write your description using the five questions above as a guide. As you begin each installment, check your timeline to get some ideas on how life might have changed by that year. Begin each installment with an appropriate variation of this sentence:

It is now _____ and I am _____ years old.
        (year)

98 Unit IV

Organize your autobiographical sketch by answering in sequence the five questions on page 98. Since you'll probably find it easier to visualize yourself and your life-style at age twenty-five, begin there. Use your earlier guesses about the future to give you a sense of possibilities for change across the decades. With each installment, be ready to make a bigger imaginative leap into the future. Concentrate not just on how the world might change but how you will change with it. Concentrate on how you might shape your own future.

When you have finished both installments of your future autobiography, read back through them. In what part of your life do you anticipate the most change over the next thirty-plus years? Will the biggest changes be in the place you live, the kind of dwelling, your family situation, your work, or your recreation? Compare the biggest area of change you foresee with those predicted by your classmates.

Going Beyond

Remember that you are going to look into your future. Reconsider the five questions you thought about previously. Choose one of the following options for producing your future autobiography:

- Make a three-chapter booklet, appropriately titled. Include your timeline as an appendix. An appendix is a separate part at the end of a publication.
- Attach your time line and both installments of your autobiography to a large piece of posterboard. Title and illustrate your display. Be sure to add your name and age.

Future Wheels

The events of our world are remarkably interrelated. When something important happens, a domino effect often follows as one event triggers another. When railroad tracks were laid across the American prairie, for example, life changed forever in the West. Communication improved because trains delivered the mail. Cattlemen and ranchers could move their beef to markets in the Northeast. Towns grew along the railroad tracks and people moved west. But not all of the consequences of railroads were so positive. The huge herds of buffalo were quickly slaughtered for sport or profit. And since the railroads ran across lands which had been the home of Native Americans, the railroad helped to displace Native Americans from their homes.

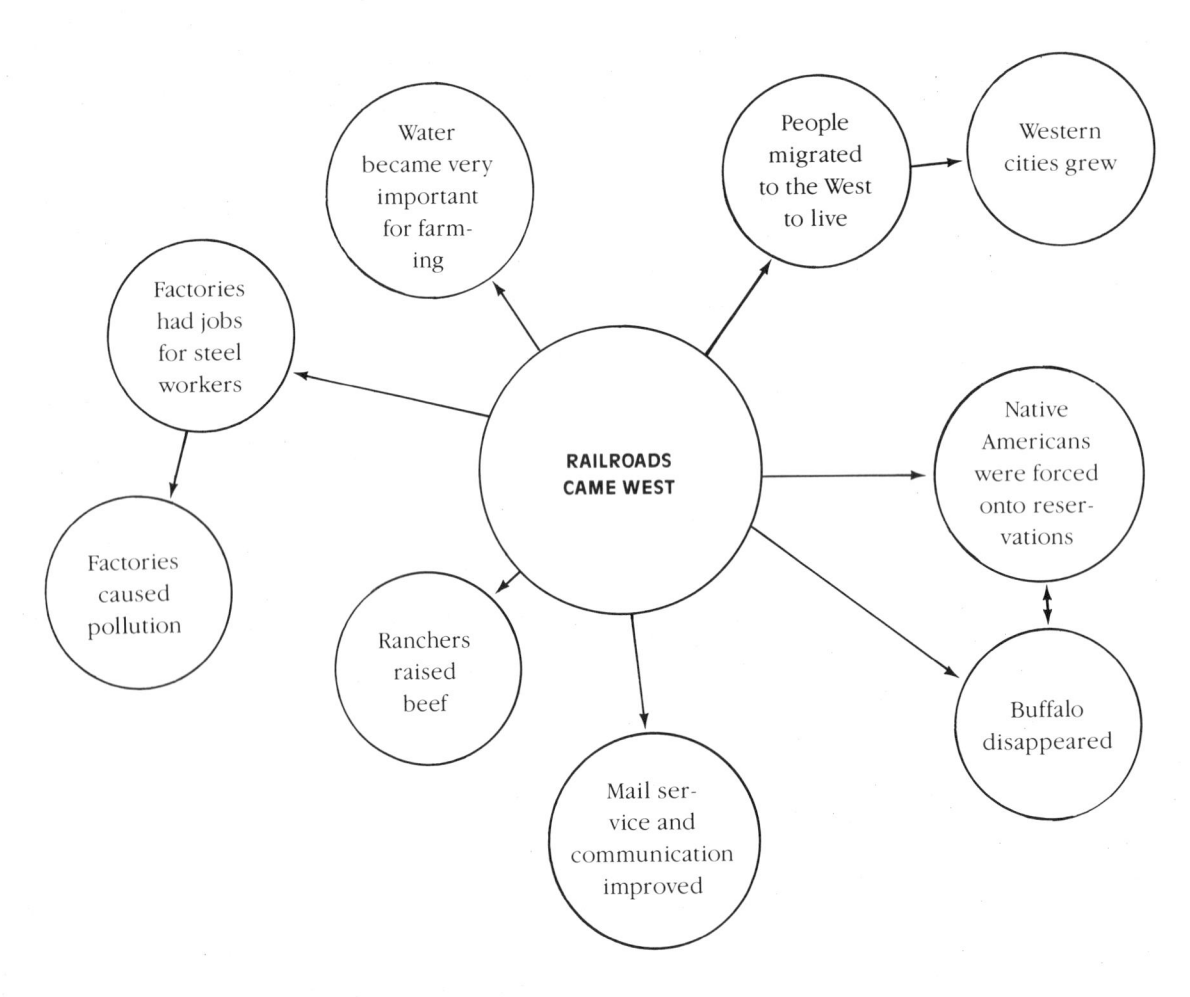

(Diagram: Central node "RAILROADS CAME WEST" with arrows to: Water became very important for farming; People migrated to the West to live → Western cities grew; Native Americans were forced onto reservations ↔ Buffalo disappeared; Mail service and communication improved; Ranchers raised beef; Factories had jobs for steel workers → Factories caused pollution)

ACTIVITY

Making A Future Wheel

ON YOUR OWN

1. Think about how life has changed since the 1930s when the airplane became a safe and reliable means of travel. Use a future wheel such as the one below to list resulting changes, both positive and negative. Draw arrows to illustrate how some things are related to others.

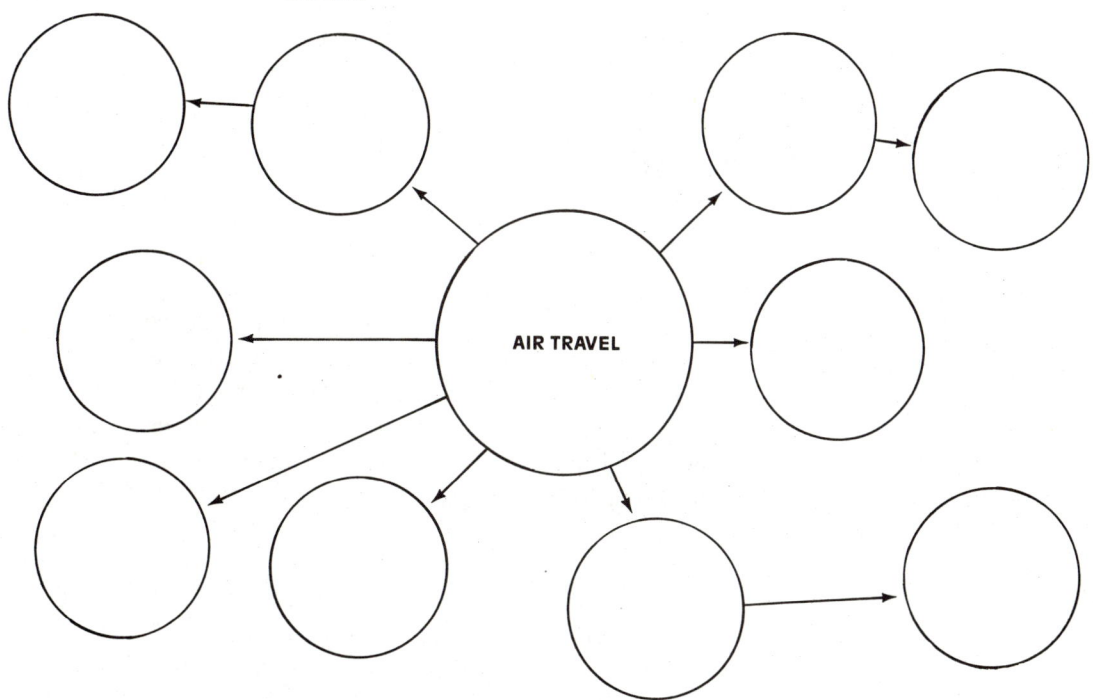

2. Now that you have practiced making a future wheel, select an event you expect to happen in the future. You might choose one of the changes you placed on your time line during the forecasting exercise. Place that event in the center and construct a future wheel illustrating possible consequences of that change. Above each result that you consider positive, put a plus. Above any that you consider negative, put a minus.

IN A GROUP

Compare your future wheel with those of several classmates. Consider the changes explored by members of your group. Which of the many possible changes in the future do you think will have the most impact on our lives? Do you see anything ahead which might change our lives as much as the automobile or electricity?

Probing the Future

ACTIVITY
Taking Stock

ON YOUR OWN

Before getting started on your project for this unit, take a few minutes to think about what you've done so far. One good way is to sift through your futures file and study what you've collected. Besides assorted clippings, you should have quite a bit of work. Has doing the work helped you see some new possibilities in your future? Keep those possibilities in mind as you get ready to write your own version of what life will be like in the future.

ACTIVITY
Fictionalized Forecast

Futurists and science fiction writers are particularly fond of creating stories of what life will be like in the future. These stories, usually called scenarios, are written by imagining how changes in technology and values may affect our lives. Ray Bradbury is a writer who has written about the future for many years. He wrote the following scenario for the year 2026.

ON YOUR OWN

As you read the short story, notice Ray Bradbury's imaginary technologies. How many of these creations are possible today?

You may find the vocabulary in this story a bit challenging. Keep a list of words that are strange or interesting to you. You may want to check into these words later.

August 2026:
There Will Come Soft Rains

In the living room the voice-clock sang, *Tick-tock, seven o'clock, time to get up, time to get up, seven o'clock!* as if it were afraid that nobody would. The morning house lay empty. The clock ticked on, repeating and repeating its sounds into the emptiness. *Seven-nine, breakfast time, seven-nine!*

In the kitchen the breakfast stove gave a hissing sigh and ejected from its warm interior eight pieces of perfectly browned toast, eight eggs sunnyside up, sixteen slices of bacon, two coffees, and two cool glasses of milk.

"Today is August 4, 2026," said a second voice from the kitchen ceiling, "in the city of Allendale, California." It repeated the date three times for memory's sake. "Today is Mr. Featherstone's birthday. Today is the anniversary of Tilita's marriage. Insurance is payable, as are the water, gas, and light bills."

Somewhere in the walls, relays clicked, memory tapes glided under electric eyes.

Eight-one, tick-tock, eight-one o'clock, off to school, off to work, run, run, eight-one! But no doors slammed, no carpets took the soft tread of rubber heels. It was raining outside. The weather box on the front door sang quietly: "Rain, rain, go away; rubbers, raincoats for today. . ." And the rain tapped on the empty house, echoing.

Outside, the garage chimed and lifted its door to reveal the waiting car. After a long wait the door swung down again.

At eight-thirty the eggs were shriveled and the toast was like stone. An aluminum wedge scraped them into the sink, where hot water whirled them down a metal throat which digested and flushed them away to the distant sea. The dirty dishes were dropped into a hot washer and emerged twinkling dry.

Nine-fifteen, sang the clock, *time to clean.*

Out of warrens in the wall, tiny robot mice darted. The rooms were acrawl with the small cleaning animals, all rubber and metal. They thudded against chairs, whirling their mustached runners, kneading the rug nap, sucking gently at hidden dust. Then, like mysterious invaders, they popped into their burrows. Their pink electric eyes faded. The house was clean.

Ten o'clock. The sun came out from behind the rain. The house stood alone in a city of rubble and ashes. This was the one house left standing. At night the ruined city gave off a radioactive glow which could be seen for miles.

Ten-fifteen. The garden sprinklers whirled up in golden founts, filling the soft morning air with scatterings of brightness. The water pelted windowpanes, running down the charred west side where the house had been burned evenly free of its white paint. The entire west face of the house was black, save for five places. Here the silhouette in paint of a man mowing a lawn. Here, as in a photograph, a woman bent to pick flowers. Still farther over, their images burned on wood in one titanic instant, a small boy, hands flung into the air; higher up, the image of a thrown ball, and opposite him a girl, hands raised to catch a ball which never came down.

The five spots of paint—the man, the woman, the children, the ball—remained. The rest was a thin charcoaled layer.

The gentle sprinkler rain filled the garden with falling light.

Until this day, how well the house had kept its peace. How carefully it had inquired, "Who goes there? What's the password?" and, getting no answer from lonely foxes and whining cats, it had shut up its windows and drawn shades in an old-maidenly preoccupation with self-protection which bordered on a mechanical paranoia.

It quivered at each sound, the house did. If a sparrow brushed a window, the shade snapped up. The bird, startled, flew off! No, not even a bird must touch the house!

The house was an altar with ten thousand attendants, big, small, servicing, attending, in choirs. But the gods had gone away, and the ritual of the religion continued senselessly, uselessly.

Twelve noon.

A dog whined, shivering, on the front porch.

The front door recognized the dog voice and opened. The dog, once huge and fleshy, but now gone to bone and covered with sores, moved in and through the house, tracking mud. Behind it whirred angry mice, angry at having to pick up mud, angry at inconvenience.

For not a leaf fragment blew under the door but what the wall panels flipped open and the copper scrap rats flashed swiftly out. The offending dust, hair, or paper, seized in miniature steel jaws, was raced back to the burrows. There, down tubes which fed into the cellar, it was dropped into the sighing vent of an incinerator which sat like evil Baal in a dark corner.

The dog ran upstairs, hysterically yelping to each door, at last realizing, as the house realized, that only silence was here.

It sniffed the air and scratched the kitchen door. Behind the door, the stove was making pancakes which filled the house with a rich baked odor and the scent of maple syrup.

The dog frothed at the mouth, lying at the door, sniffing, its eyes turned to fire. It ran wildly in circles, biting at its tail, spun in a frenzy, and died. It lay in the parlor for an hour.

Two o'clock, sang a voice.

Delicately sensing decay at last, the regiments of mice hummed out as softly as blown gray leaves in an electrical wind.

Two-fifteen.

The dog was gone.

In the cellar, the incinerator glowed suddenly and a whirl of sparks leaped up the chimney.

Two thirty-five.

Bridge tables sprouted from patio walls. Playing cards fluttered onto pads in a shower of pips. Martinis manifested on an oaken bench with egg-salad sandwiches. Music played.

But the tables were silent and the cards untouched.

At four o'clock the tables folded like great butterflies back through the paneled walls.

Four-thirty.

The nursery walls glowed.

Animals took shape: yellow giraffes, blue lions, pink antelopes, lilac panthers cavorting in crystal substance. The walls were glass. They looked out upon color and fantasy. Hidden films clocked through well-oiled sprockets, and the walls lived. The nursery floor was woven to resemble a crisp, cereal meadow. Over this ran aluminum roaches and iron crickets, and in the hot still air butterflies of delicate red tissue wavered among the sharp aroma of animal spoors! There was the sound like a great matted yellow hive of bees within a dark bellows, the lazy bumble of a purring lion. And there was the patter of okapi feet and the murmur of a fresh jungle rain, like other hoofs, falling upon the summer-starched grass. Now the walls dissolved into distances of parched weed, mile on mile, and warm endless sky. The animals drew away into thorn brakes and water holes.

It was the children's hour.

Five o'clock. The bath filled with clear hot water.

Six, seven, eight o'clock. The dinner dishes manipulated like magic tricks, and in the study a *click*. In the metal stand opposite the hearth where a fire now blazed up warmly, a cigar popped out, half an inch of soft gray ash on it, smoking, waiting.

Nine o'clock. The beds warmed their hidden circuits, for nights were cool here.

Nine-five. A voice spoke from the study ceiling:

"Mrs. McClellan, which poem would you like this evening?"

The house was silent.

The voice said at last, "Since you express no preference, I shall select a poem at random." Quiet music rose to back the voice. "Sara Teasdale. As I recall, your favorite...."

"There will come soft rains and the smell of the ground,
And swallows circling with their shimmering sound;

And frogs in the pools singing at night,
And wild plum trees in tremulous white;

Robins will wear their feathery fire,
Whistling their whims on a low fence-wire;

And not one will know of the war, not one
Will care at last when it is done.

Not one would mind, neither bird nor tree,
If mankind perished utterly;

And Spring herself, when she woke at dawn
Would scarcely know that we were gone."

The fire burned on the stone hearth and the cigar fell away into a mound of quiet ash on its tray. The empty chairs faced each other between the silent walls, and the music played.

At ten o'clock the house began to die.

The wind blew. A falling tree bough crashed through the kitchen window. Cleaning solvent, bottled, shattered over the stove. The room was ablaze in an instant!

"Fire!" screamed a voice. The house lights flashed, water pumps shot water from the ceilings. But the solvent spread on the linoleum, licking, eating, under the kitchen door, while the voices took it up in chorus: "Fire, fire, fire!"

The house tried to save itself. Doors sprang tightly shut, but the windows were broken by the heat and the wind blew and sucked upon the fire.

The house gave ground as the fire in ten billion angry sparks moved with flaming ease from room to room and then up the stairs. While scurrying water rats squeaked from the walls, pistoled their water, and ran for more. And the wall sprays let down showers of mechanical rain.

But too late. Somewhere, sighing, a pump shrugged to a stop. The quenching rain ceased. The reserve water supply which had filled baths and washed dishes for many quiet days was gone.

The fire crackled up the stairs. It fed upon Picassos and Matisses in the upper halls, like delicacies, baking off the oily flesh, tenderly crisping the canvases into black shavings.

Now the fire lay in beds, stood in windows, changed the colors of drapes!

And then, reinforcements.

From attic trapdoors, blind robot faces peered down with faucet mouths gushing green chemical.

The fire backed off, as even an elephant must at the sight of a dead snake. Now there were twenty snakes whipping over the floor, killing the fire with a clear cold venom of green froth.

But the fire was clever. It had sent flames outside the house, up through the attic to the pumps there. An explosion! The attic brain which directed the pumps was shattered into bronze shrapnel on the beams.

The fire rushed back into every closet and felt of the clothes hung there.

The house shuddered, oak bone on bone, its bared skeleton cringing from the heat, its wire, its nerves revealed as if a surgeon had torn the skin off to let the red veins and capillaries quiver in the scalded air. Help, help! Fire! Run, run! Heat snapped mirrors like the brittle winter ice. And the voices wailed. Fire, fire, run, run, like a tragic nursery rhyme, a dozen voices, high, low, like children dying in a forest, alone, alone. And the voices fading as the wires popped their sheathings like hot chestnuts. One, two, three, four, five voices died.

In the nursery the jungle burned. Blue lions roared, purple giraffes bounded off. The panthers ran in circles, changing color, and ten million animals, running before the fire, vanished off toward a distant steaming river....

Ten more voices died. In the last instant under the fire avalanche, other choruses, oblivious, could be heard announcing the time, playing music, cutting the lawn by remote-control mower, or setting an umbrella frantically out and in the slamming and opening front door, a thousand things happening, like a clock shop when each clock strikes the hour insanely before or after the other, a scene of maniac confusion, yet unity; singing, screaming, a few last cleaning mice darting bravely out to carry the horrid ashes away! And one voice, with sublime disregard for the situation, read poetry aloud in the fiery study, until all the film spools burned, until all the wires withered and the circuits cracked.

The fire burst the house and let it slam flat down, puffing out skirts of spark and smoke.

In the kitchen, an instant before the rain of fire and timber, the stove could be seen making breakfasts at a psychopathic rate, ten dozen eggs, six loaves of toast, twenty dozen bacon strips, which, eaten by fire, started the stove working again, hysterically hissing!

The crash. The attic smashing into kitchen and parlor. The parlor into cellar, cellar into sub-cellar. Deep freeze, armchair, film tapes, circuits, beds, and all like skeletons thrown in a cluttered mound deep under.

Smoke and silence. A great quantity of smoke.

Dawn showed faintly in the east. Among the ruins, one wall stood alone. Within the wall, a last voice said, over and over again and again, even as the sun rose to shine upon the heaped rubble and steam:

"Today is August 5, 2026, today is August 5, 2026, today is . . ."

ACTIVITY

Bradbury Revisited

WITH A PARTNER

Talk the story over with a classmate. Talk especially about the technologies Bradbury built into his scenario.

1. At what point in the story did you realize that the house was empty and that the voices were really machines?

2. What details made you feel as if you were in the house and could see and hear exactly what was going on?

3. Which of these technologies do you think will really be possible by the year 2026? Which ones do you think might never be possible?

Probing the Future

4. You'll remember that on your future wheel, you predicted the consequences of some big change. You marked those consequences with pluses and minuses according to whether they were positive or negative. In Bradbury's story, what positive results of technology do you see? What destructive results?

ACTIVITY

Starting Your Own Scenario

Ray Bradbury wrote "There Will Come Soft Rains" in 1950. Like many others at that time, he was concerned with the way technology could destroy the human race.

Now it's time for you to start a story showing the way you see the future. In some ways, your story will be like Bradbury's. You'll take some trend, technological change, or world event that could bring about dramatic change. You'll imagine your story taking place in a particular year in the future. Of course, your story won't be as long and elaborate as Bradbury's, and it probably won't be as grim.

You may develop your story any way you wish. Maybe something as simple as the effect of technological changes on education could provide the kernel idea. A student in 2025 coming home from school could provide the setting. Maybe it's only 11:00 A.M. because on Tuesday he or she goes to school only long enough to meet with a discussion group. Maybe she or he finds electronic messages on a screen indicating where everyone is and maybe the student goes upstairs to an electronic desk and does schoolwork on some kind of computer linked to the school. You may not be thrilled with this story kernel, but you get the idea. To turn that idea into a first-rate scenario, a writer would need to add as many specific details as possible—things like what the messages said and what his room looked like.

ON YOUR OWN

Jot down some ideas for a story. If you are stuck for a way to get started on your story, follow these steps:

- Decide on what major change you want to dramatize in your story. Jot down as many specific details as you can about that change.
- Decide on the year of your scenario. You may want to return to your trusty time line again for an idea.

- Consider several places which might serve as the setting for your story: a home, a school, a shopping center, a factory, a farm, a nonearth location.
- What about characters for your scenario? You will recall that Bradbury didn't use any humans. In the book *2001: A Space Odyssey* one of the main characters is a computer named HAL. One piece of advice—keep it simple and don't get your story cluttered with characters.
- Try beginning your scenario by setting the scene in much the same way Bradbury did.

WITH A PARTNER

Before you actually begin writing your story, talk your ideas through with a partner. Try spinning out a scenario based on your ideas as you thought through the steps above. Be imaginative and specific. See what your partner likes best, and ask for suggestions. Tell the story again and see how it sounds.

ON YOUR OWN

Get your scenario on paper. At this time, don't fuss over word choice or punctuation. Just concentrate on telling your story from start to finish. Try to bring your vision of the future to life with lots of detail. When you finish, put your paper aside for a while. A little time-out will help you step back and see the story from a fresh perspective. Then you can do a better job of shaping it into final form.

Going Beyond

Read more scenarios about the future. Here are some good places to start:

- Find a copy of Ray Bradbury's *The Martian Chronicles*. Read selected stories or the whole book.

- Thumb through a recent issue of *Omni* magazine. Read at least one article and one short story about the future.
- Browse through the science fiction section of your library. Check out a novel you think you'll enjoy reading.

Futurists' Forum

You'll remember that the art festival and the technology fair you held earlier didn't just happen. They took lots of planning. So will the futurists' forum you'll be hosting in a few days.

This time the planning should be easier. You've had some practice in this important kind of thinking. You've learned to divide a big job into several smaller ones. You've also learned to sequence and coordinate those tasks. That's exactly what you'll do in planning the futurists' forum.

ACTIVITY

Organizing the Forum

> AS A CLASS

First, you'll need your teacher's help in setting a date. Then take a few minutes to think about what a forum accomplishes and how it's run.

A forum brings people together to exchange information and ideas on an important issue. It usually begins with several prepared presentations which spark give-and-take discussion among participants. Ideas flow freely as people speak out on a subject of special interest and expertise. You can see why futurists find forums so informative and stimulating.

To organize your class forum, you'll need four committees to start work right away. Form committees to meet and make plans to complete the following tasks:

1. PROGRAM—When scenarios have been put in final form, the program committee will read and select the five most interesting and original ones to be read aloud at the futurists' forum. Besides getting a chair to preside and arranging to have each reader introduced, this committee will also choose five students to serve as a panel and respond to each scenario after it is read. You can start right away on this.

2. PUBLICATIONS/EXHIBITS—This committee will arrange to have scenarios not presented at the forum reproduced in a souvenir booklet, bound into one scrapbook to be kept in the classroom, or displayed on an appropriately illustrated bulletin board. First, the committee should explore these options and confer with the teacher about which is most feasible. Later, the committee will oversee the process of publishing or otherwise displaying scenarios.

3. INVITATION—The first job of this committee will be to decide what special guests should be invited to the class forum. Besides the school principal and faculty, think of other adults with a strong interest in the future—for example, city planners and professors from any nearby universities who teach courses about the future. The next job is to write invitations and keep track of replies.

4. ROOM ARRANGEMENTS—If you aren't expecting too many guests, the forum can be held right in your own classroom. In this case, the room arrangements committee will just need to be sure there's a podium for presenters and a table for panelists. Seating may be arranged auditorium style or in semicircular rows. This committee may also want to set the tone by constructing a futurists' forum poster, perhaps with a suitable theme or quotation and high-tech illustrations.

AS A GROUP

When your committee meets, you'll probably want to select a chair as you have done during previous projects. Then you can make a chronological list of jobs to be done and decide which committee members will be responsible for each. You may want to make a chart summarizing assignments and deadlines as you did in planning the art festival. (See page 32.) Again, you'll want to check off tasks as they are completed and keep your teacher posted. Since committees must coordinate their work, chairs will need to stay in close touch.

ACTIVITY

Shaping Up Your Scenario

Now that work on the forum is underway, it's time to put the finishing touches on your own contribution.

WITH A PARTNER

Read your scenario aloud to a partner and ask for responses to these questions:

1. Have I set the scene so that you get a clear picture of time and place? Do you also get a clear picture of what the future might be like as a result of the change described in the story?
2. Is there anything I need to tell more about?
3. What parts do you like best?
4. If this were your scenario, what would you do to improve it?

Probing the Future 111

ON YOUR OWN

Considering what you learned from your partner, go through your scenario and pencil in changes. As you make a final copy, check any questionable spelling or punctuation with your partner. Hand in your scenario so that it can be considered by the program committee.

ACTIVITY

Taking Part in the Forum

AS A CLASS

You may have been assigned a special part in the futurists' forum. Maybe you are one of the five presenters to read your scenario aloud or one of the five-member panel that will comment on the imaginary future pictured in each scenario. Even if you aren't on the panel, you'll have a chance to respond from the floor. You may ask questions or contribute related information from your own futures file or ideas from your own scenario. You may also comment on how likely or unlikely various scenarios are to come true or on ways scenarios are alike and different. The point is to exchange as many thoughts about the future as possible.

Thinking like a Futurist

At the beginning of this unit, we said that thinking like a futurist is a little like daydreaming. Like inventors, futurists must take imaginative leaps, as you did in writing your scenario. Didn't imagination also help in creating your metaphor for the future?

Imagination is one of the futurists' most valued tools, but it's not the only one. There's also the ability to predict, forecast, and project consequences. Those are important kinds of thinking. All planning depends on looking ahead.

Can you see ways that thinking like a futurist can help you in school? Can you see how this kind of thinking will help later as you adapt to a world that is changing so fast it almost makes us dizzy?

ACTIVITY

Mind Metaphors

At the end of each previous unit, you've taken time to reflect on your own work. More importantly, you've reflected on how your mind *did* that work. In other words, you've thought about your own thinking. Now it's time to reflect on how you thought through various tasks in this unit.

> **ON YOUR OWN**

Sift through your futures file one more time and try to remember how you did each piece of work. What seemed especially easy and natural? Where did you get stuck? How did you get unstuck? Did you learn more from one project than from others?

You may also want to think back to earlier units. Do you see any patterns in the way your mind seems to work through all kinds of tasks? What kinds of thinking do you do best? What kinds of thinking always seem tough?

It's hard to understand something as complicated as thinking, especially thinking that goes on inside your own head. In this unit, you've learned that one way to understand something hard is to think what it's *like*. That's why your final reflection will be an exercise in metaphor.

Take a few minutes to think about these three devices:

- a filing cabinet
- a computer
- a video camera

What does each device do? How does it work? Consider each separately and jot down notes as you go. In what ways do you think your mind works like each device? In what ways does it work differently?

Which of these devices makes the best metaphor for how your mind works? Maybe you can think of another metaphor for a mind—an X-ray, a strainer, or a kaleidoscope. Develop that metaphor on paper. Begin with the sentence "My mind is like a _____."

The first few sentences of Chad's reflection may help you get the idea:

My Mind

My mind is like a filing cabinet. Since I have such a good memory, my head is always full of things I've seen, heard, and read. I'm pretty well organized, too. That's like putting new facts and ideas in the right folder.

A file cabinet is mainly full of papers with words on them. I like to think in words. Sometimes I draw pictures, but it's really writing things down that helps me figure them out.

Later, Chad goes on to say how his mind is *not* like a filing cabinet.

Try a similar approach in writing your own mind metaphor. Tell how your mind works like the device you've chosen and how it works differently.

IN A GROUP

Share your reflection with others who chose the same metaphor. As reflections are read, jot down all the ways different people see their minds working like a file cabinet or a computer or a video camera. Which items on each list echo something you said in your paper? Why did you leave out the other items? Which did you just not think of? Which don't really apply to you?

Talk through these questions with the rest of the group. Together, choose one paper to read aloud to the rest of the class. Write on the chalkboard your group's list of ways members' minds are like and unlike the device you chose as a metaphor.

AS A CLASS

Have the paper selected earlier read aloud. Report highlights of your group discussion and invite questions about the list on the chalkboard.

After all groups have reported, study the three lists and recall the discussion about each metaphor. What are the advantages of having a mind like a file cabinet, like a computer, like a video camera, or other mind metaphors?

What can your mind do that none of these devices can? As you finish this book, we hope you've only begun to answer that question. Keep up the mental exercise!